BRITAIN IN OLD PHOTOGRAPHS

NORTHALLERTON

A SECOND SELECTION

MICHAEL RIORDAN

SUTTON PUBLISHING LIMITED

Sutton Publishing Limited
Phoenix Mill · Thrupp · Stroud
Gloucestershire · GL5 2BU

First published 1998

British Library Cataloguing in Publication Data
A catalogue record for this book is available from the British Library.

ISBN 0-7509-1807-1

Typeset in 10/12 Perpetua.
Typesetting and origination by
Sutton Publishing Limited.
Printed in Great Britain by
Ebenezer Baylis, Worcester.

CONTENTS

Arnold Pearson was born on a farm near Newby Wiske, educated at Northallerton Grammar School and has lived in Northallerton virtually ever since, giving outstanding service to the community as the resident even-handed reporter on the *Northern Echo* and *Darlington and Stockton Times* for thirty years; for an equal time an Independent and caring North Riding County Councillor for the Romanby/Brompton Ward, with the eventual honour of being made an Honorary Alderman; and for many years the ultra-involved Chairman of the Northallerton Royal Air Force Association. Sandwiched in this is a distinguished war record as a member of the Royal Air Force Volunteer Reserve from 1940 (aged nineteen) to 1945. Flying with Bomber Command as an Air Gunner/Wireless Operator he survived sixty-seven bombing missions mainly in Lancasters, latterly with No. 7 Squadron as a member of the famous Pathfinder Force, flew with three VC winners as his pilot, became a Squadron Leader and was awarded the gallantry medals of DSO and DFC. He is totally unassuming. Married to Gladys for well over fifty years, with two children and grandchildren, he is a dedicated family man whose thoughts are often with his young flying friends who never returned.

INTRODUCTION

Northallerton's history, founded on eighteen centuries of existence, is already well documented. However, the anatomy of the North Yorkshire county town will continue to be dissected, investigated and reported. Indeed, Northallerton has so many different facets with each one a fascinating study.

It is essentially a historic town probably with Roman origins and consolidated in the Saxon period, for it was a fully fledged Saxon settlement with sixty-six freemen, twenty-one surrounding villages in its jurisdiction and a Saxon stone church before the Norman conquest of 1066.

As a route centre commanding the main eastern passage between England and Scotland Northallerton became important not only in local but in national terms. During the Anglo-Scottish Wars waged for three centuries it was central to innumerable English advances and some actions, including the famous Battle of the Standard in 1138, many royal visits of English kings and Scottish invasions, one of which (in 1314) saw the town and church burned.

In more peaceful times it was a major town on the busy Great North Road and then on the main east coast railway line, commencing in 1841. It was throughout the ages an ecclesiastical and a political centre: Northallerton parish church dominated the town and area continually; the parish sent two members to parliament in 1298 and then regularly between 1640 and 1832 when it was reduced to one member, and though it lost this seat in 1885 it remained the centre and 'returning' town for the Richmondshire constituency.

Northallerton had always been an administrative and judicial centre and became the county town of the North Riding in the eighteenth century when the Registry of Deeds (1736), the County Court House (1783) and the County Gaol (1785) were built there. This was substantiated when the North Riding County Hall was sited on the old Northallerton Racecourse in 1903 and confirmed when North Yorkshire was instituted in 1974.

Finally, with agriculture at the very basis of Northallerton's existence, it was fundamentally a farming and market town. Its very name indicates this – 'Alfhere's tun' or Alfred's farm was its original name derivation – in Saxon times its freemen had had thirty ploughs, weekly markets were held from medieval times and by 1610 it had been granted four annual fairs by Royal Charter which had acquired a national reputation especially for their cattle and later horses.

Indications of all Northallerton's main characteristics are evident in this volume's collection of photographs, as too are other traits and its complementary features.

For example, for centuries the town had been renowned as an 'ale town'. In 1851 there were twenty-seven public houses down the main street and previously Giles Morrington in his poem of 1697 'In praise of Yorkshire Ale' wrote:

'Northallerton, in Yorkshire, does excel
All England, nay all Europe, for strong ale.'

It had also developed strong hospital traditions with St James' richly endowed and widely known hospital established in about 1200 on the outskirts of the town up the Thirsk road. The Maison Dieu (1476) and Rutson (1877) hospitals followed and the crowning hospital glory was the Friarage, which grew from eight wooden huts in 1940 to a magnificent modern hospital complex.

Education too has been a forte as Northallerton boasts one of the oldest grammar schools in the north of England back to at least 1322 when Robert Colstan was the Master, and which has prospered this century to become the now vigorous and forward looking Northallerton College. The Allertonshire School as one of the first ever secondary modern schools in 1941 became a national and international educational showpiece. And from a 'sand desk' in the Vicarage coach house in 1841 for ordinary children have developed, including Brompton and Romanby, seven modern and stimulating primary schools. (The 'sand desk' was a large table topped with sand where the children learned to write their letters and figures. They then graduated to the more expensive copybooks when they were more proficient.)

The thriving town has produced a vibrant social life which has manifested itself in entertainment and sport. A Georgian Theatre was built in 1800 in Tickle Toby yard and this dramatic and entertainments lead has been followed by many societies and groups, culminating today with for example the Amateur Operatic Society, the Amateur Variety Company and the Allerton Players.

In 1612 Robert Hackforth of Deighton was fined for 'playing at boules within the Churchyard' which emphasises the keen interest in sport in the district. Northallerton had a racecourse from 1765 which every October until 1880 held a lucrative and popular race meeting. It also had a reputation for the games 'spell and knurr' and cricket in the eighteenth century, and when sports were popularised in the nineteenth century all the main sports flourished and multiplied. Rugby football, association football and cricket were rapidly organised and developed along with many other sports. The abundance of sporting photographs in this volume illustrates the importance to which sport was accorded by the local people.

This is an apt allusion to finish with – because people were and are the core of Northallerton's existence: people living everyday lives every day for nearly two millennia.

CHAPTER ONE

THE HISTORIC TOWN

Northallerton High Street is pictured arrestingly in the later nineteenth-century pre-motor car era in its cobbled state, with the narrower made-up road running down to the market around the Town Hall. Here we are looking at a scene that is part of national history. Situated on the main eastern route between England and Scotland, almost equidistant between London and Edinburgh, Northallerton has been in a vitally important position through the ages. Always central to the town has been the High Street, which was involved in every military movement in the centuries-long turbulent Anglo Scottish Wars, after which in more peaceful times it was an essential part of the Great North Road, up and down which the main stage-coaches plied. Locally it was the trading hub of the surrounding area from time immemorial, with Wednesday markets and four annual fairs, for which the Royal Charter dates from 1200.

A bronze age battle axe discovered on the Solberge estate near Northallerton earlier this century. It belongs to businessman John Willis of Sowber Gate, and along with a bronze age spear found on Castle Hills in the 1890s it is the most ancient artefact discovered in the Northallerton district. Made of basalt, it is very heavy, of remarkable craftsmanship for the time and dates from between 1500 and 800 BC.

All Saints' church has been at the centre of Northallerton and its affairs for around 1,200 years. Its baptistry, photographed in 1951, is Early English; the font dates from 1662, when it was restored after the English Civil War, and bears the initials of the vicar Thomas Mann and his four churchwardens. A recent addition on the western wall is the Roll of Honour to the Northallerton Fallen of the Second World War, 1939–45, dedicated in 1949.

This monument, familiar to travellers on the Northallerton to Darlington road, was erected in 1913 to commemorate the famous Battle of the Standard, fought in the very early daylight hours of 22 August 1138, 3 miles north of Northallerton. It is on the western side of the battlefield and was subscribed to by local people on the initiative of bank manager W. S. Charlton. In the fierce and bloody battle the English routed the Scots, who suffered very heavy losses.

A market cross has existed at Northallerton from medieval times, probably originally adjacent to the churchyard and more recently farther south in the High Street. When the butchers' shambles were demolished and replaced by the town hall in 1873, the market cross was sold to Percival Hindmarsh for £5 and was then removed to John Jefferson's garden at Standard House, where it stood until 1913 when he gave it to the town. It is seen here in that year being re-erected just to the south of the town hall.

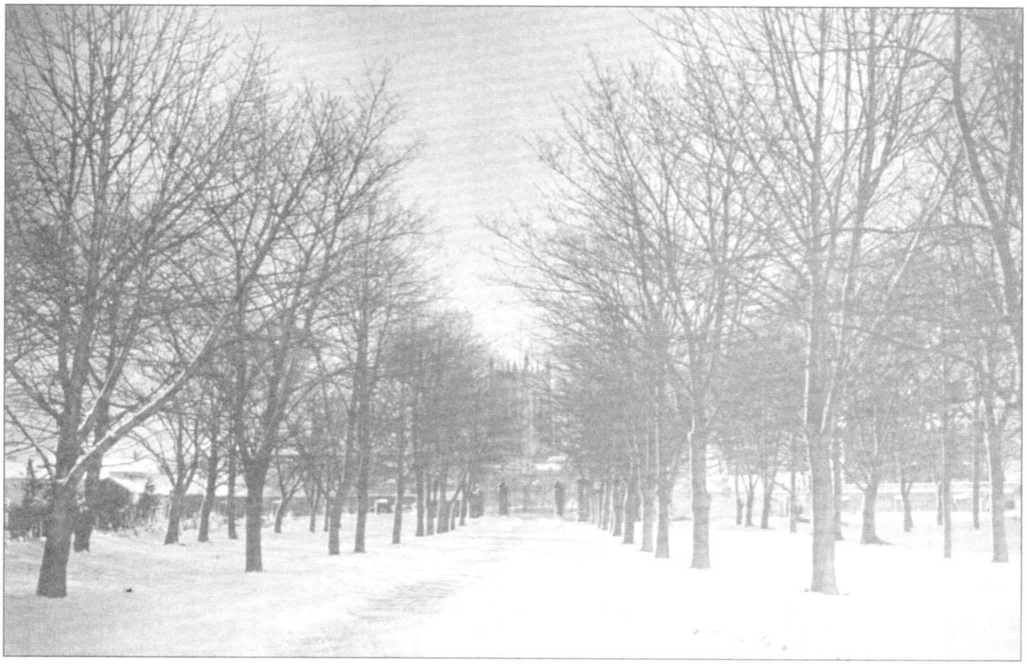

The scenic entry to Northallerton cemetery is captured in winter, *c.* 1900. This was a famed path in Northallerton history, because it was the entrance to the Bishop of Durham's Palace which stood on the cemetery site from 1200 to 1663. During this time numerous well-known people including royalty passed down this road – for example, King John, Edward I, Edward II, Edward III and Princess Margaret in 1502. She was en route to marry King James IV of Scotland: this union led to the merging of the English and Scottish thrones under James I of England in 1603.

These large old building stones were unearthed some years ago when a grave was being prepared in Northallerton cemetery, and undoubtedly belong to the Bishop of Durham's Palace once sited here. There is also the possibility that they belonged originally to Northallerton Castle. This was built in 1130 on Castle Hills, but such was its dominance that King Henry II ordered it to be 'overthrown and laid level to the ground' in 1176. Many of its stones were used to build a smaller alternative acceptable to the king – the Bishop of Durham's Palace.

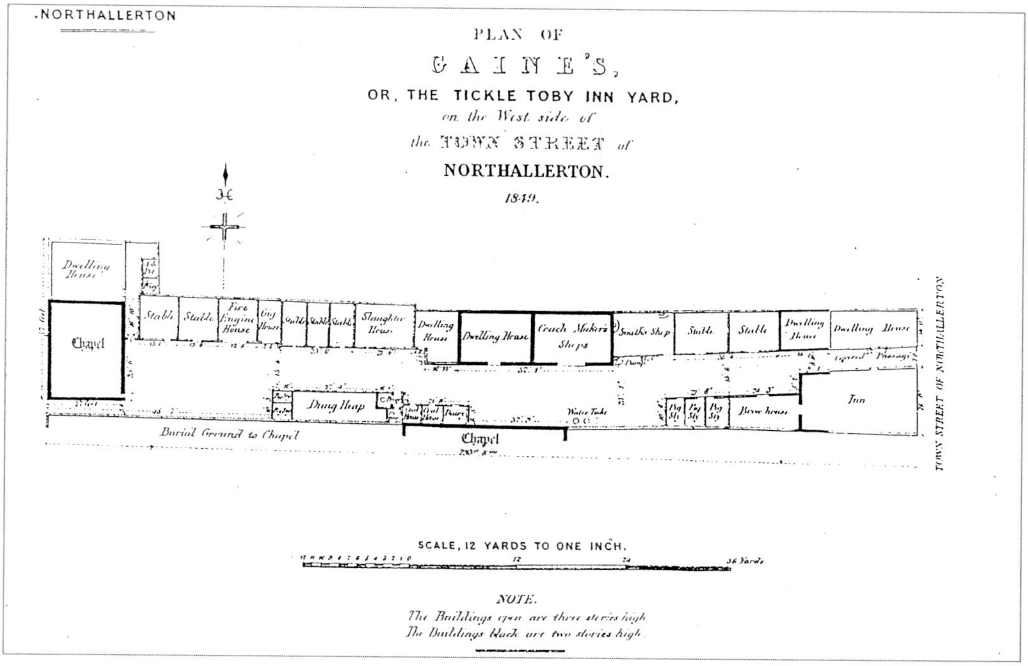

This plan of the Tickle Toby yard is invaluable as it was the only detailed plan of a yard given in the 1849 Report of the Local Government Board of Health into the sanitary and living conditions of Northallerton. Conditions were appalling in most of the yards off the High Street, with half the town's population of 3,000 living in them. That this was one of the better yards speaks volumes, for privies, a dung heap, stables, pigsties and a slaughterhouse existed cheek by jowl with the inhabited houses, with the fire engine house and an adjacent graveyard thrown in for good measure!

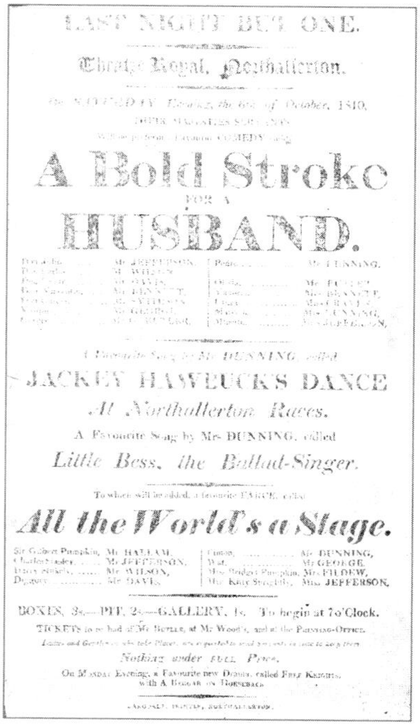

LAST NIGHT BUT ONE.

Theatre Royal, Northallerton.

On SATURDAY Evening, the 6th of October, 1810,

A Bold Stroke FOR A HUSBAND.

A Favourite Song by Mr DUNNING, called

JACKEY HAWEUCK'S DANCE

At Northallerton Races.

A Favourite Song by Mrs DUNNING, called

Little Bess, the Ballad-Singer.

To which will be added, a favourite FARCE, called

All the World's a Stage.

Sir Gilbert Pumpkin,	Mr HALLAM,	Cimon,	Mr DUNNING,
Charles Stanley,	Mr JEFFERSON,	Wat,	Mr GEORGE,
Harry Stukely,	Mr WILSON,	Miss Bridget Pumpkin,	Mrs FILDEW,
Diggory	Mr DAVIS,	Miss Kitty Sprightly,	Miss JEFFERSON,

BOXES, 3s.—PIT, 2s.—GALLERY, 1s. To begin at 7 o'Clock.

TICKETS to be had of Mr Butler, at Mr Wood's, and at the Printing-Office.

Nothing under FULL Price.

On Monday Evening, a Favourite new Drama, called Free Knights, with A Beggar on Horseback

The chapel indicated at the end of the Tickle Toby yard was originally built in 1800 as the Theatre Royal by drama impresario Samuel Butler, as one of five in a circuit that included the Georgian Theatre, Richmond. He alternated his troupe of dramatis personae at the different theatres, Northallerton's turn always occurring in early October to coincide with the town's prestigious three-day race meeting. This theatre bill of 6 October 1810 substantiates this, but after Butler died the Theatre Royal declined and it was sold to the Primitive Methodists in 1834. It became their chapel until 1891.

NORTHALLERTON BOROUGH ELECTION, 1874.

Sir,

Mr. GEORGE W. ELLIOT begs to draw your earnest attention to the following

INSTRUCTIONS TO VOTERS.

1. Vote **EARLY**, to prevent your opponents voting in your name.
2. On going into the Polling Booth you will be asked your name and where you live. A Ballot Paper will then be given you, and you will have to go into a private box, where you will find a pencil. You must then place a X on the RIGHT hand side of the Ballot Paper, opposite the name of Mr. ELLIOT, (being the first name on the paper) as in the form below.
3. You must, on no account, make any other mark on the Ballot Paper. If you do, your vote will not be counted.
4. Fold up the Ballot Paper and put it into the Ballot Box.
5. If you should accidently spoil a Ballot Paper, you must give it to the Presiding Officer, and he will give you another.

FILL UP THE VOTING PAPER THUS:

1	**ELLIOT,** (GEORGE WILLIAM, Langton Hall, Northallerton, Yorkshire; and Penshaw House, Fence Houses, Durham).	X
2	**WRIGHTSON,** (WILLIAM BATTIE, Cusworth Park, near Doncaster, Yorkshire).	

The Election will take place on **TUESDAY,** 3rd February.

This cleverly constructed poster was on behalf of Conservative George W. Elliot (the new linoleum factory owner), who was contesting the Borough of Northallerton seat in 1874 with the Liberal William B. Wrightson. It was the first ever election by secret ballot and for the first time the powerful land and property owners could not directly influence the voter's intentions; therefore they had to use more subtle methods. Every vote was vital because Elliot only won by nine votes in the ensuing election – 387 to Wrightson's 378. Northallerton had an imposing political pedigree, first sending two MPs to Parliament in 1298 and then two continually from 1640 to 1832, when it lost one member with the Great Reform Act. In 1885 Northallerton lost the privilege of its own MP, when it was merged with Richmond into the Richmondshire constituency.

CHAPTER TWO

PEOPLE & PLACES

The parade of the Northallerton detachment of the National Reserve to the north of the Town Hall, 30 June 1913. This organisation had just been formed and was similar to the later Home Guard; it afforded a local defence force of volunteers who could not join the regular armed services or Territorial Army. It was very popular and was commanded by Walter G Eaton. Of interest are the fashions of the onlookers, the buildings in the background and the absence of cars, bicycles being the 'in' transport! The buildings are, left to right, the Mason's Arms and outbuildings; the post office on the corner of Friarage Street (now Hunt and Wrigley's, solicitors), open from 8 a.m. to 8 p.m. Mondays to Saturdays with Post Master Joseph Chatterton; the Yorkshire Penny Bank, open Wednesdays 10 a.m. to 4 p.m., Saturdays 10 a.m. to 4 p.m. and Saturdays 6 p.m. to 8 p.m.; and Wheldon and Co., drapers.

Northallerton's first mart with top-hatted clientele, 1874. Atkinson's opened in 1873: before this date all animals had been sold in the High Street. Behind the pens on what is now the main County Hall site is Northallerton Racecourse with its grandstand, which flourished from 1765 to 1880. At the top left is the original building of the Railway Hotel and Posting House, formerly the Horse and Jockey and then added to in Swiss chateau style by Dan Oakley and Co. Ltd in 1901. Later it was given its present name, the Station Hotel.

Alfred Bourne owned the Railway Hotel after it was altered and kept horses in the field across the road that has recently been developed with residential houses. Known as Bourne's Field, it arouses affectionate memories amongst the older generation of hilarious, tingling sledging in the winter and cricket in the summer, when the railway station staff XI played there. Alfred was one of the best-known men locally at the turn of the century as he also owned two other renowned establishments – the Queen Catherine, Osmotherley, and during and after the First World War the Golden Lion, Northallerton, which he is pictured standing outside in 1920. The Golden Lion had a national reputation, and stabled working horses: these operated coaches from the hotel to the railway station and delivered mail.

There were two other public houses named Railway in 1900; both were on the east side of the North End main road. The Railway Hotel was the furthest north, near to the North End railway crossing, and the Railway Inn was farther south: it is now re-named The Standard. Standing outside the Railway Inn in about 1930 are the resident Lumley family, parents and children: left to right: Gordon, Emma (landlady), Mary, John (landlord), Lillian and Ted. Mary later married Harry (Joe) Render, the renowned Northallerton cricketer.

Interspersed with the yards which led off the High Street were many spacious gardens, leading on the west side from commodious High Street-facing houses right back to the Applegarth. One of these is seen here in about 1910: it is Barclays Bank's garden, with bank manager Thomas Russell, his wife, Marian (née Baines), and children, Harriet (left) and Hilda. Thomas was the first Barclays and Co. manager after it combined with Backhouse and Co. in the early 1900s, and lived there in Bank House with his family. The daughters later became very accomplished artists, having pictures hung locally and nationally. With modern development the garden, like many of the others, is now used as a car park.

Sun Beck used to run open down Bullamoor Road, then down Friarage Street on its southern side. It often flooded, causing chaos even in the 1950s, when an early Friarage hospital worker recalls being rescued from a watery ward by Willy Wake's coal waggon. In a memorable photograph here of the 1931 floods a car is manfully tackling flooded Friarage Street past the Baptist chapel, and in the background schoolchildren outside the East Road National School are 'splodging' in the flooded beckwaters – a fondly remembered schoolchild's pastime.

Ernest Gardner, portrayed here in the 1890s, was born into fame because he was the son of Captain George Gardner, a gallant survivor of the Battle of Balaclava – one of the Six Hundred – and governor of Northallerton Gaol for twenty-nine years from 1862. Ernest was himself a man of many parts. He qualified as a solicitor, married Cicely Jefferson, the daughter of Northallerton's leading attorney John Ingelby Jefferson, and with her had two children, Dudley and Grace Gardner (who became well known in their own right), became Northallerton's foremost solicitor and the coroner for the North Riding of Yorkshire, was elected on to the Urban District Council of which he became chairman, and rose to become the Commanding Officer of 'H' (Northallerton) Company of the 4th Battalion Green Howards Territorials by 1910. Ernest was also one of the most accomplished local amateur actors and entertainers.

While most of Northallerton's yards were in a dire state in the nineteenth century, the advent of running water alleviated matters and several yards were comparatively congenial by the middle of the twentieth century. This leafy study on a sunlit day of Fairburn's yard, which went from the east side of the High Street near the Black Bull back to East Road, certainly creates a good impression.

Holidays abroad were hardly thought of in Northallerton during the 1920s and 1930s, but pleasant times were had with nostalgic memories of such places as Scarborough and Blackpool. The family of John and Annie Boston spent happy days in Blackpool and here in the late 1920s the two elder of their four daughters are photographed in a Blackpool studio. Dorothy is on the left with Gwen mounted on a worthy steed!

On Sundays and Bank Holidays families used to stroll around the town and its environs after the traditional Sunday dinner, and Castle Hills was a favourite spot for people of both Northallerton and Romanby in the 1930s and before. Girls in white ankle socks and frocks, ladies with hats and gentlemen in suits and ties – all in their Sunday best – are recalled. Mr and Mrs Kingston of Romanby are seen here resting on Castle Hills on a sunny Sunday afternoon in 1934 with, left to right, their daughters Eileen (six), Doreen (two) and Nita (four).

Sunday schools were very much the vogue before the Second World War and the Wesleyan church Sunday school at the north-eastern end of the High Street flourished considerably. Here a group of its young girls pose for the camera in 1938. Back row, left to right: Mr Chatterton, -?-, Marjorie Hancock, -?-, Dorothy Cowell, ? Blakey, Miss Lee, -?-. Second row: Sheila Tiffany, Margot Garlick, -?-, Dorothy Hall, -?-, -?-, Mary Plows. Front row: Rosamund Farndale, -?-, Kathleen Hutchinson, Dorothy Watson, Dorothy Garlick, Dorothy Palliser, Sylvia Cowell, Amy Watson, Dorothy Holmes, Gladys Watson.

The southern end of the east side of the High Street has seen considerable physical change since this photograph in the early 1960s. The Primitive Methodists built and opened this chapel in the 1890s and it prospered for years as the South End Methodist church before closing in the 1960s, when Romanby Methodist church opened because of the shift of population. The chapel is now lost to High Street view and Naylor's garage and petrol pumps have disappeared along with those of Smirthwaite's just to the south – although the latter has moved to East Road. James Naylor and Thomas Smirthwaite ran two of the main garages in Northallerton and both had premises here on the High Street before 1905.

Informal photographs of Northallerton's yards just before the redevelopment of the back of the High Street are very informative, and in this striking example from 1954 three little boys are safely playing on the cobbles in the Liberal Club Yard on the western side of the High Street. Renee's Hairdressers was at the end near to what is now Boots the Chemists. The boys are, left to right, Brian Lawson, Michael Durham, and John Spence. Moira Ware is walking towards them.

One of the most popular resorts of the young people of Northallerton and Romanby from about 1948 onwards was the Youth Club, held at Allertonshire School. This photograph dates from 1951. Back row, left to right: Don Cranston, Harold Young, Mr Cousins (Youth Leader), -?-, Derek Fawcett. Third row: Peter Vickerton, -?-, Vernon Tennant, John Severs, John DiPalma, Michael Sturgiss, -?-, Michael Metcalf. -?-, -?-, -?-, -?-, Colin Nicholson, Brian Glasper, Maurice Macintosh, -?-, Mick Riordan, Walter Lonsdale. Second row: -?-, -?-, Jean Blakey, Yvonne Aconley, Dorothy Bainbridge, Kathleen Horner, Thelma Lacey, Peggy Peacock, Pam Hutchinson, Winnie I'Anson, Rhoda Chapman, -?-. Front row: Valerie Cappleman, Joy Simpson, Gillian Henderson, Joyce Kirtley, -?-, Barbara Dunning, -?-, Sheena Wilson, Dorothy Sunter, Olga Sunter.

The Lyric Cinema was opened in October 1939 with the film *We're going to be Rich*, starring Gracie Fields, having been newly built by Walter Thompson Ltd on the demolished site of Bowman's and White's yards. Until it closed in June 1995 it served the town and district well, and here old age pensioners are enjoying a charity concert in the early 1950s. Front row, left to right: Mrs Kingston, Mrs Archer, Mrs Clemmet, Mrs Smart. Second row: Mrs Playforth, Mrs Fenton, Mrs Burley, Mrs I'Anson. In 1998 the New Life Baptist church purchased, converted and re-opened the building as their church.

CHAPTER THREE

THE COUNTY TOWN

North Riding of Yorkshire county business had been conducted in Northallerton since Tudor times and the building of the register office in Zetland Street (1736) followed by the North Riding house of correction (1783) and court house (1785) established Northallerton as the county seat. But it was the erection of the county hall building, seen here shortly after it was built in 1903, that confirmed Northallerton's position as the North Riding and then the North Yorkshire (1974) county town. The building has been added to frequently since: for example, the north wing (1916), south wing (1930) and a joining wing (1940); there have been considerable additions since. Obviously the county town status has had an enormous influence on the character, structure, history, economy and development of Northallerton. In each separate area – roads, architecture, education, finance, law and order, for example – a fascinating story exists. And the human element has been crucial. An extra group of people has been brought in to enhance the town both socially and economically. Some sporting and social photographs are a reminder of this human interest.

One of the original chief clerks at the county hall, Mr Frederick Pinkney, is pictured behind his desk in the new county hall in about 1906 in the days of ledgers, parchment and ink pens – if not quite quills! Before the county building was opened in 1906 a comparatively small number of offices were spread through the town in thirteen different places, including upstairs rooms in what is now the Station Hotel. Note Mr Pinkney's high winged collar: the dress code was of the highest standard, in keeping with the immaculate copper-plate writing.

With the county hall in place at Northallerton North Riding County Council soon erected other county buildings in Racecourse Lane: a police headquarters (1909), a new registry of deeds (1927) and finally a new court house in 1936, the opening of which is seen here. North Riding Quarter Sessions had been held at Northallerton intermittently since 1555, and permanently after the old court house was built in 1785. The clerk of peace for these and clerk to the county council, Hubert G. Thornley, is standing at the back right of the photograph. He was knighted in 1958 to local and national acclaim for his services to the North Riding.

The North Riding Police Force was a vital aspect of the county council's remit, and by the time this photograph was taken in 1955 police conveyances had developed from horse-drawn carriages and then bicycles to Ford Zephyrs, controlled from a magnificent new police division traffic headquarters in Racecourse Lane. Seated in this car outside the Tan Hill pub is PC Joe Tarporley; it is believed that because of the altitude he may be out of range of radio transmissions!

Sport was a major recreation amongst North Riding County Council employees, especially the police force, and the measure of encouragement and interest from the top can be gleaned from the number of senior officers seen with this successful Police HQ and Road Traffic Division team of 1954/5. Back row, left to right: Mr Smithers (Civilian), PC Jim Woodward, PC Mike Horner, PC Roberts, Cadet Lyons, PC George Paley, the referee. Centre row: Superintendent 'Nobby' Clarke, Assistant Chief Constable H.H. Salisbury (later Chief Constable), PC Ernie Woodward (Captain), Superintendent Bingent, Detective Inspector Milnes. Front row: Cadet Ferguson and Cadet Mike Green.

The official county staff union, the National Association of Local Government Officers (NALGO), consistently had an excellent cricket team, and in this 1947 XI every player had represented Northallerton CC 1st XI. The team was pictured on the old Northallerton Racecourse Lane ground in front of the ancient wooden pagoda pavilion, and it contained Albert Gaskell who later became nationally known as a first class umpire in the county championship. Back row, left to right: Albert Gaskell, Sam Wilkinson, Alan Pearson, C. Tapling. Front row: John Broadley, Walter Couling, Les Spence, Ray Fawcett, Brian Dawson, Denys Cooper, Frank Lowther.

The North Riding Education Committee staff are seen here at their Christmas party, held in the Golden Lion Assembly Rooms, 1953. Seated in the second row from the front is Frank Barraclough, the county education secretary of national repute (centre, wearing glasses) with his wife to the right; she was aunt of Richard and David Attenborough of media fame. Others in the photograph are the Coverdale twins, John and Arthur, with Don Wood (back row, extreme right); Terry McLean and Jean Mason (back row, extreme left) who later married; Brian Wallace, Phyllis Elliot and Joan Stevens (middle); and J.W. Clarke, Harry Mitchinson and Bill Pearson (front row, right).

Six of these ladies were the first females to be employed in the North Riding Education Department other than those with degrees or professional qualifications. This was in the later 1930s, when they became clerks or typists. It was the idea of Frank Barraclough, the forward-thinking secretary to the education committee. Left to right: Olive Challans, Linda Manging, Bessie Randall, Christine Ewbank, Edith Marchant, Dorothy Lancaster, Jenny Dodds, Belle Smith.

In the 1950s an annual friendly cricket match was played between the North Riding education staff and the Northallerton Grammar School and staff at the school. Here are the teams together in 1951. It was always a competitive but a most enjoyable occasion. Back row, left to right: Harold Oddy, Colin Nicholson, Nick Jobling, Bill Hallett, A.T. Richardson, David Peter, Arthur Arrand, Geoff Husband, Bill Pearson, John Wood, Bill Lowther, Geoff Lyall, -?-, Jack Clark. Middle row: Doug Metcalfe, John Boynton, Mick Riordan, Roger Hartley, Harry Mitchinson, John Palmer, Don Wood. Front row: Donald Richardson, Ernold Cuthbert, Reg Welburn, Brian Glasper.

Whenever a general election took place members of the North Riding of Yorkshire staff acted as electoral officers, overseeing the correct conduct of the election for the Richmondshire constituency. This group, photographed in 1957, is organising the ballot boxes at Northallerton Town Hall, where the votes were counted and the result was announced from the balcony by the returning officer. Left to right: Frank Smith, Bill Robinson, Doug Metcalfe, -?-, John Palmer, Ronnie Kirk, Dick Fletcher.

The county hall staff had frequent social gatherings, the major ones including Christmas or spring balls held in Northallerton. Here is a typical photograph taken at the county hall spring ball at the Golden Lion Hotel, Northallerton, in 1958. Left to right: Don Watson, Rosemary Harrison, Joan Cawthorne, Joan Boyes, Margaret Watson, Kath Atkinson, Jean Johnson, Barry Cawthorne.

Chapter Four

A Hospital Town

On 11 October 1877 a cottage hospital with six beds was opened at Northallerton in the building on the High Street called Vine House – as it had once sported the most extensive vine in Europe. In 1903 Henry Rutson of Newby Wiske entered the hospital as a patient with afflicted eyesight, and this experience moved him to endow the hospital with its Vine House building, and later to add the house next door to the north and a substantial financial donation. The hospital adopted his name of Rutson, and his philanthropy ranks high in the remarkable Northallerton hospital tradition – which goes back to the medieval hospital of St James in 1200 and forward to today's modern Friarage Hospital.

Here are two unusual hospital-related photographs. From 1939 to 1988 the Northallerton District Maternity Hospital was The Mount, a large late-Georgian house on the northern outskirts of the town. Thus practically every child born in this period from the area was born at The Mount, which became a local household name. The ornately furnished room seen here was the drawing room of The Mount when it was a private country house owned by John Weston Adamson. He leased it in 1939 to serve as the North Riding's maternity home, and sold it as such in 1945.

The Friarage Hospital is built on the site of a former Carmelite friary dating from 1356 – hence the name. Evidence of this occurred in February 1954 when this skeleton was unearthed as Priory Close was being built on the edge of the hospital. The burial ground of the Carmelites had been discovered there in 1888, when several perfect skeletons were found.

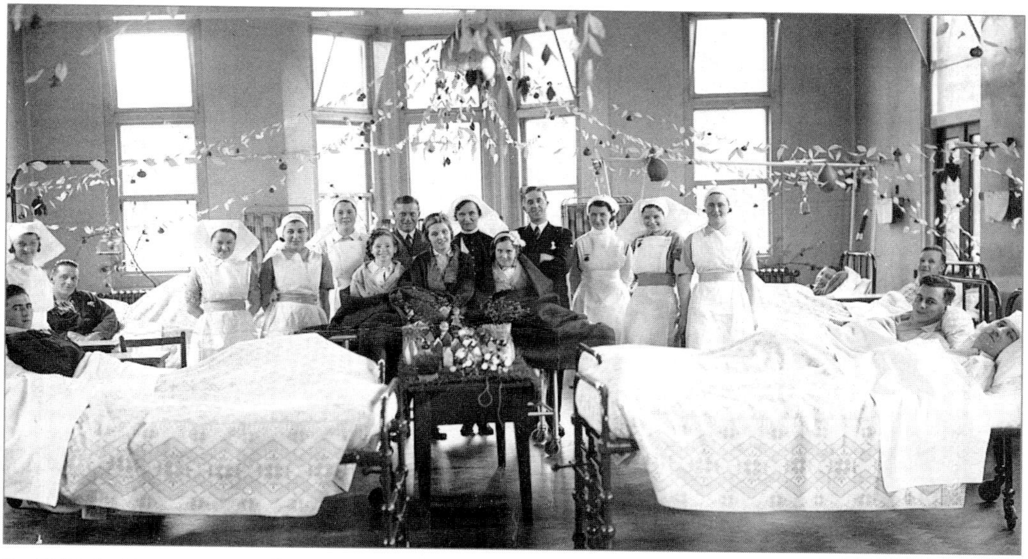

By 1936 the Rutson Hospital had prospered enormously since 1885, when the acquisition of a tin bath had caused great excitement there. A new wing in 1932 had doubled the capacity to twenty-eight beds, and new equipment including X-ray provision had been obtained. Equally important, it was a happy place with a congenial atmosphere, as can be gauged by the smiling faces in this photograph of the new male ward at Christmas 1936. All the nursing staff are present, with the matron Miss S. Hall standing at the back between Dr Davey (left) and Dr McKenzie, who were two of the main GP users. John Burn of Brompton is in the bed at the back on the right.

When the Friarage was re-opened as a civilian hospital in 1948, an orthopaedic nurses training school was immediately set up, followed in January 1949 by a state registered nurses school with a cadet scheme for sixteen year olds. By 1959 147 nurses had qualified, with the supply of home-grown nursing staff vital to the hospital's development and its happy and friendly reputation. Additionally some SRNs went far afield to Malaya, Hong Kong, Canada, South Africa, Aden, Singapore and Japan. Here a nurses' class is concentrating on an anatomy lesson conducted in the old workhouse building, Sunbeck House, where their school was accommodated in the 1950s.

Children's care was a Friarage speciality. Here, staff and children in Children's Ward 10 are admiring flowers sent by the Love Apple League and flown from Guernsey to Royal Air Force Yeadon (now Leeds/Bradford Airport), 1955. Staff, left to right: Staff Nurse Robinson, Nurse Plant, Nurse Piggins, Sister Rhea.

An annual event at the Friarage Hospital in the 1950s took place every Christmas Day, when Gerry Wilson, the choirmaster, brought the parish church choir to the hospital after matins to sing carols from ward to ward. Such occasions as this are nostalgically recalled by choirboys and men, staff and patients alike. The photograph dates from 1951.

A Friarage ball was a highlight of the hospital's social calendar, when hospital and town met. This is the ball committee in 1960. Left to right: Alan Wilson (chief administrator), Cassia Harker (matron from 1951 to 1963, who wrote *Call Me Matron*), Mrs R.A. Rawlings, Mrs Joan Cawthorne, Brenny Archer (vice-chairman, Northallerton Hospital League of Friends – later chairman, and awarded the MBE).

Since its inception in 1957 the Northallerton Hospitals League of Friends has given enormous support to the Friarage Hospital, contributing millions of pounds through the initiative, energy and generosity of people from every part of the hospital's wide catchment area. A most important annual event has been its well-attended garden fête which is shown here on Saturday 14 July 1956 – when the pony rides for children were photographed. William Barker (left) and C.H. Scott are leading and the two girl riders are Vicky Bedford (left) and Barbara Hart.

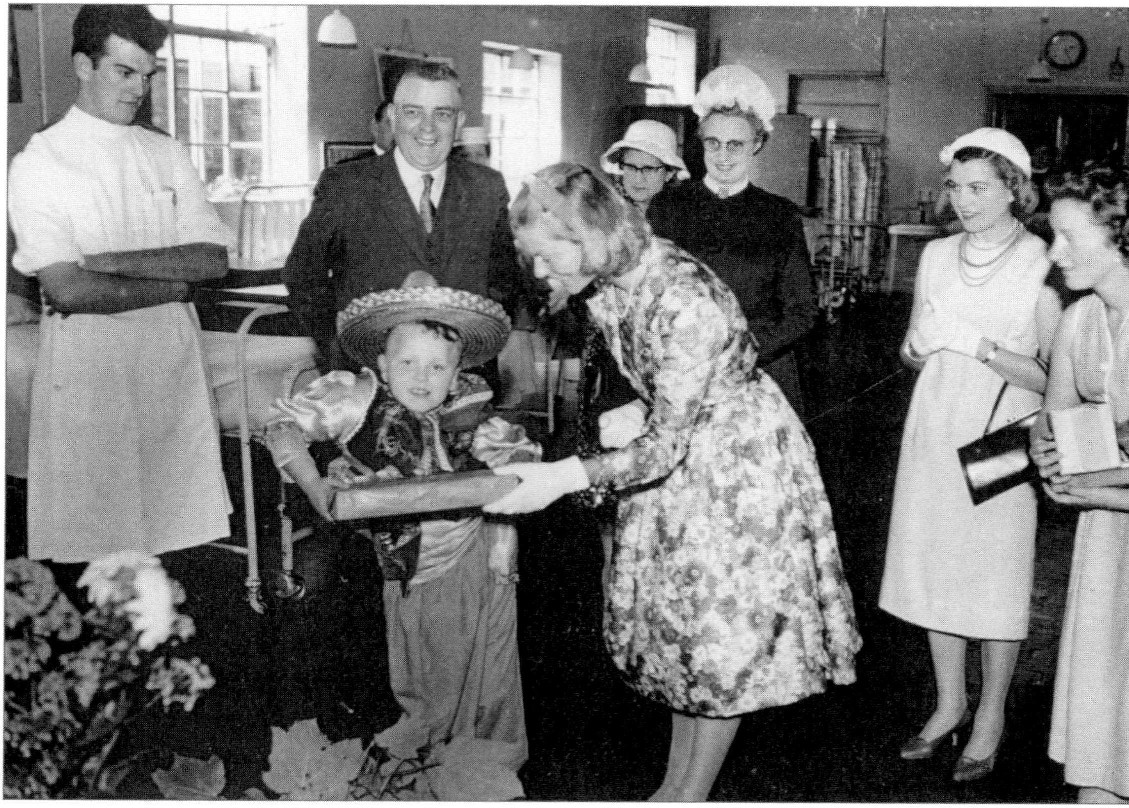

The Friarage Hospital has had a succession of important visitors during its relatively short existence, commencing whe was a Royal Air Force establishment – with actors Robert Donat and Bernard Miles and then King George VI's sister, Princess Royal, all in 1943. Ministers Leon Brittan (trade and industry) and Edwina Currie (junior health) came to o stages of the Phase I Redevelopment in the later 1980s and royalty visited latterly: the Duke and Duchess of York 2 August 1989 and Princess Alexandra in June 1992. Katherine Worsley, shown here, was not quite a royal when enchanted people at the Friarage on 20 June 1959 because it was just before her marriage to the Duke of Kent, but did not make her appearance any less memorable for everyone who met that popular lady. She is seen here presenting fancy dress first prize in the children's ward with, left to right, Nurse Bobby Cooper, 'Nobby' Clarke (later MBE), King, Matron Cassie Harker, Joan Cawthorne, -?-.

CHAPTER FIVE

NORTHALLERTON IN THE WARS

Alan Hill, the eldest son of Captain Thomas Hill (the first Chief Constable of the North Riding of Yorkshire), was born at Romanby and has the distinction of being the only holder of the Victoria Cross from the Northallerton district. He earned the VC in the early Boer War in Transvaal, South Africa, at Majuba Hill on 27 February 1881 as a Lieutenant in the 58th Northamptonshire Regiment. Under withering fire, with no regard for his personal safety, he plucked an officer to safety – but he was killed in his arms; though wounded, Hill saved another soldier and helped save the colours from being captured. He was given a hero's welcome when he returned to Romanby and later rose to the rank of Major. In 1902 Hill married Miss Muriel Lilian Oliphant Walker, the daughter of T.S. Walker of Maunby Hall, and changed his name to Hill-Walker. Despite the injuries suffered in the Transvaal he led an active life, being a zealous fox-hunter, and when he died on 21 April 1944 he was the oldest living holder of the VC. Trumpeters of the Northamptonshire Regiment sounded the last post at his funeral as he was laid to rest in the little churchyard near his Maunby home.

The horror of trench warfare on the Western Front in the First World War is legendary, and the unfortunates involved must have dreamed and longed for their homes and their loved ones. This photograph of Cpl Harry Carter of Castle Hills, taken in France in 1915, captures this exactly – as he is pictured thinking of his wife Clara and son Alastair, who are inset at the top of the photograph. Harry was in the service corps, responsible for horse transport and trench supplies, and fortunately survived the holocaust.

Ninety-eight Northallerton men who had fallen in the First World War were commemorated on the war memorial unveiled by the Lord Lieutenant of the North Riding, Sir Hugh Bell, in the ceremony recorded here on 6 August 1921. It was an impressive and deeply moving occasion because no road, yard or household was untouched by the tragic losses – a fact epitomised by the Vicar of Northallerton, the Revd S. McKinnon Thompson, who dedicated the memorial and whose son Lt Charles Thompson was killed in action in 1916, aged twenty-three.

A LAST APPEAL TO REASON
BY
ADOLF HITLER

Speech before the Reichstag, 19th July, 1940

I have summoned you to this meeting in the midst of our remendous struggle for the freedom and the future of the German ation. I have done so, firstly, because I considered it imperative o give our own people an insight into the events, unique in history, hat lie behind us, secondly, because I wished to express my gratitude o our magnificent soldiers, and thirdly, with the intention of ppealing, once more and for the last time, to common sense in eneral.

If we compare the causes which prompted this historic struggle vith the magnitude and the far-reaching effects of military events, ve are forced to the conclusion that its general course and the acrifices it has entailed are out of all proportion to the alleged easons for its outbreak — unless they were nothing but a pretext or underlying intentions.

The programme of the National-Socialist Movement, in so far as t affected the future development of the Reich's relations with the est of the world, was simply an attempt to bring about a definite evision of the Treaty of Versailles, though as far as at all possible, his was to be accomplished by peaceful means.

the world our resolution to shake off the shackles of the Versailles Dictate.

Germany's demands for this revision were a vital necessity and essential to the existence and honour of every great nation. They will probably one day be regarded by posterity as extremely reasonable. In practice, all these demands had to be carried through contrary to the will of the Franco-British rulers. We all regarded it as a sure sign of successful leadership in the Third Reich that for years we were able to effect this revision without a war. Not that — as the British and French demagogues asserted — we were at that time incapable of fighting. When, thanks to growing common sense, it finally appeared as though international co-operation might lead to a peaceful solution of the remaining problems, the Agreement to this end signed in Munich on September 29, 1938, by the four leading interested States, was not only not welcomed in London and Paris, but was actually condemned as a sign of abominable weakness. Now that peaceful revision threatened to be crowned with success, the Jewish capitalist war mongers, their hands stained with blood, saw their tangible pretexts for realizing their diabolical plans vanish into thin air. Once again we witnessed a conspiracy by wretched corruptible political creatures and money-

needed a long war, because they had now invested their capital in armaments shares, had purchased machinery and required time for the development of their business interests and the amortization of their investments. For, after all, what do these "citizens of the world" care about Poles, Czechs or such-like peoples?

On June 19, 1940, a German soldier found a curious document when searching some railway trucks standing in the station of La Charité. As the document bore a distinctive inscription, he immediately handed it over to his commanding officer. It was then passed on to other quarters, where it was soon realized that we had lighted on an important discovery. The station was subjected to another, more thorough-going search.

Thus it was that the German High Command gained possession of a collection of documents of unique historical significance. They were the secret documents of the Allied Supreme War Council, and included the minutes of every meeting held by this illustrious body. This time Mr. Churchill will not succeed in contesting or lying about the veracity of these documents, as he tried to do when documents were discovered in Warsaw.

These documents bear marginal notes inscribed by Messieurs

In the early months of the Second World War propaganda leaflets were dropped from both German and British aircraft to influence the respective civilian populations, and this is such a leaflet. It was released from a German aeroplane and found with others near Osmotherley in July 1940: this was at Britain's darkest hour, with the threat of invasion looming. In the leaflet Hitler argues the lunacy of opposing the might of Germany and advises surrender. It is extremely doubtful that he persuaded anyone around Northallerton!

Propaganda again – but this time from an advertising campaign by the British Government aimed at influencing people to invest in Saving Certificates to help the war effort, rather than wasting money and succumbing to the 'Squander Bug'. Each year during the war there was a special week earmarked for war savings. For example, in Wings for Victory week in May 1943 Northallerton's target of £80,000 was nearly doubled when £152,000-worth of National Savings Certificates were bought.

May 1941 was a particularly traumatic month, especially for the children of Northallerton. On the night of 12–13 May Northallerton was bombed by a lone German plane, which dropped four high explosive and a cluster of incendiary bombs. The latter started a quickly extinguished fire at the county hall, and one of the HE bombs sliced through the White House (right) on the west side of South Parade, which has since been demolished and replaced by Stanley Court. A soldier killed here was the only fatality of the entire raid – the first victim of warfare in Northallerton for several centuries.

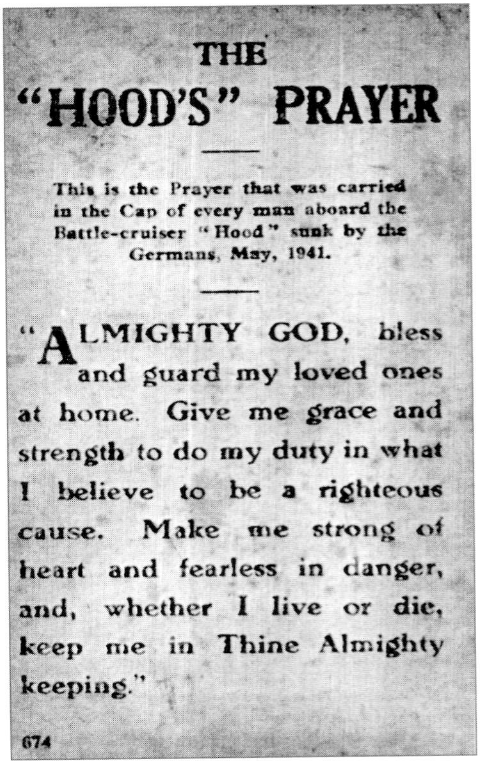

THE
"HOOD'S" PRAYER

This is the Prayer that was carried in the Cap of every man aboard the Battle-cruiser "Hood" sunk by the Germans, May, 1941.

"ALMIGHTY GOD, bless and guard my loved ones at home. Give me grace and strength to do my duty in what I believe to be a righteous cause. Make me strong of heart and fearless in danger, and, whether I live or die, keep me in Thine Almighty keeping."

674

On 24 May 1941 the battleship HMS *Hood*, the pride of the British Fleet, was sunk by a direct hit on the magazine by the *Bismarck* with the loss of all but three of its crew of 1,418. This was shattering news, greeted with numbed disbelief by the children at Northallerton's Applegarth School – who had adopted the *Hood*, sent crates of gifts and comforts and acquired close pen pals. The poignant '*Hood*'s Prayer' reproduced here was composed by Applegarth School and carried by every crew member. The loss was almost too hard to bear for the young children, aged only five to nine.

This is not a cosmonaut or a man from outer space but Jack Wilson, a county hall official by day but a member of the Air Raid Precaution (ARP) squad by night, dressed in his anti-gas suit in 1942. Hubert Thornley, the clerk to the county council, was county controller of air raid precautions, which though only occasionally called into action was highly organised and enthusiastic.

Several special events took place during the Northallerton Wings for Victory Week in May 1943, one of which was a grand parade from Thirsk Road through the town to the North End. One of the many participant organisations in the parade was the Girls Training Corps, seen here swinging smartly down Thirsk Road and approaching the High Street. Kay Oxley, Moira Finkill, Betty Bateson and Mary Robinson are in the ranks.

Arnold Pearson, wireless operator/air gunner who was then a flying officer, is seen outside Buckingham Palace witł fiancée Gladys and his parents, Mr and Mrs Pearson of Newby Wiske, on the occasion of his presentation with Distinguished Flying Cross by the Duke of Gloucester. By this time Arnold had completed over thirty operations, with the rest of his crew was selected to serve in the elite Pathfinder Force with No. 7 Squadron, flying Lancasters.

The Canadian connection was marked during Second World War in the area because of the presence of the No. 6 (Bomber) Group Royal Canadian Air Force from 1 January 1943. RC Leeming was particularly associated with the town, with its Halifax bombers from 427 (Lio and 429 (Bison) squadrons flying over almost nightly on bombing missions, and the crews making the most of their off-duty time there. Canadians found adoptive families who made them totally at home, and many married the lo girls they met. Carter's Farm at Castle Hills w regular haven for one group, who pose here w their hosts. Left to right: Barney Baker, Sgt Alastair Carter (RAF), Don Walters (Canada), Jack Trim (Canada), John ? (Canada).

14 October 1943 Her Royal hness the Duchess of Gloucester ted RCAF Leeming, mainly to pect the Women's Auxiliary Air ce of which she was nmandant. She is walking ween the WAAF ranks ompanied by Squadron Officer ce Litman, i/c WAAF at RCAF ming.

ming was attacked on isolated occasions by lone German aircraft during the Second World War, but it was only bombed e. This incident was on 12 July 1943: two airmen and an airwoman are surveying the huge bomb crater at the aerodrome imeter, probably with relief that the bombing was not more accurate. The sacrifice at Leeming was great, as in only two rs (1943–5) the Canadian 427 and 429 Squadrons lost 161 Halifax bombers and 903 aircrew. Their courage was immense they received 232 decorations for bravery.

On the afternoon of 11 August 1944 a reigning monarch visited RCAF Leeming. Queen Elizabeth is seen here inspecting the WAAF personnel. She had accompanied King George VI, who was simultaneously decorating eighteen Canadian aircrew and then being shown Halifax 'U' Uncle, which had had three bombs dropped on it over the target (fuselage, wing and tail fin) but had been safely flown home by the pilot, Flying Officer Murphy of 427 (Lion) Squadron, to whom the King spoke. Princess Elizabeth was with her parents at the station and Princess Margaret Rose joined them later when the royal party went to Northallerton railway station to entrain for the north. News of their presence had spread like wildfire through the town and a very large crowd gathered to greet and send them off with excited and affectionate acclamation. This was certainly a local red letter day.

An open day was held by RCAF Leeming on 16 June 1945 in the way of a thank you for its enormous local civilian support in grim and exacting times, to celebrate the end of the European war and mark the departure of the Canadians who were soon going home. People flocked to the station, and this photograph gives a sense of the occasion and of the Canadian–North Riding bond that had been established. Superintendent 'Nobby' Clarke and his family are being entertained by Canadian Flight Lieutenant Bill Hay, befriended with his pals at their home for the past two years. Left to right: Mrs Lucy Clark, Jean Clarke (aged nine), Flight Lieutenant Bill Hay, Superintendent 'Nobby' Clarke, Mrs Bean, Deputy Chief Constable Bean, Mrs Rawlings (RCAF Leeming commandant's wife).

There was great national relief and rejoicing when the unconditional surrender of Germany ended the Second World War in Europe, and this was reflected in festivities throughout the land on VE Day, 8 May 1945. The spirit of happiness was captured here at Romanby, where a party for the village children was held on the green. Among those celebrating were Jean and Yvonne Aconley, Joan Almond, Jane Groves, Brian Kell, Nita, Doreen and Gerald Kingston, Amy Watson, Olga Nicholson, Geoffrey and Lewis Lancaster, Rosamund, Peter and Alistair Vickerton, Brian Stockdale, Jimmy Critchley, Jean Calvert, Mr Aconley, Mr Almond, Mr Ellery and Mr Lancaster.

The overwhelming, unavoidable and harsh reality of the two world wars in Northallerton and district, as it was through every city, town, village and community in the nation, was the loss of life – mainly young vibrant life. Harry Megginson of Maycroft, Malpas Road, Northallerton, epitomises this stark tragedy. Simply, he attended the Applegarth and National Schools, went straight from school to his first job at the Vale of Mowbray Factory at Leeming Bar, was called up at eighteen, drafted into the Cameronians (Scottish Rifles), and in the final drive by the Allies into Germany was killed on 16 February 1945 – eleven days after his nineteenth birthday.

Harry's military grave is seen here: he lies with seven thousand of his comrades, the white commemorative stones row upon row like attentive sentinels, at the Riechwald Forest Cemetery in Germany, just over the Dutch border and between the villages of Kleve and Coch. The War Graves Commission keeps the graves immaculately as it does throughout the world, where many of Harry's Northallerton townsmen lie. The epitaph on his grave is apt for all of them: 'GREATER LOVE HATH NO MAN THAN THIS, THAT A MAN LAY DOWN HIS LIFE FOR HIS FRIEND'.

CHAPTER SIX

A COMMERCIAL TOWN

From its earliest days Northallerton has been a market and commercial centre, culminating this century when on the basis of an official report of 1953 it was tagged in the national press as 'the richest town in the country'. Certainly businesses have flourished, and one of the oldest in town is Barker's, which evolved from Oxendale's – seen here in the latter part of the nineteenth century. John Oxendale started this well-appointed business in 1875 and indentured William Barker, a farmer's boy from Cowton, as an apprentice in 1883. William rose to become a partner in 1907, when the shop was re-named Barker and Oxendale, and by 1920 he was the sole owner of the premises, then called William Barker's.

JOHN OXENDALE,

DRAPER AND OUTFITTER,

MARKET PLACE, NORTHALLERTON,

Has always in stock a large assortment of

GENERAL DRAPERY,

At the Lowest Prices; also a choice lot of

LADIES' JACKETS, ULSTERS, SHAWLS,

AND WOOL WRAPS,

Together with an Immense Stock of

READY-MADE CLOTHING,

CONSISTING OF

Boys', Youths', and Men's Suits.
Boys', Youths', and Men's Cloth Trousers.
Boys', Youths', and Men's Cord Mole & Printed Mole Trousers.
Men's Waterproof Coats.
Men's Overcoats and Munsters.
Boys' and Youths' Overcoats and Munsters.
Reefer, Pea and Pilot Jackets.
Dux, Drabett, and Velveteen Jackets.

HATS, CAPS, SCARVES, COLLARS, GLOVES,
MUFFLERS, UMBRELLAS, &C., &C.

For four decades *Smithson's Almanack* was published annually at Christmas as a digest of Northallerton life. The *Almanack* carried advertisements placed by the main businesses, and this is John Oxendale's entry of 1881. Later, under William Barker and his son Leslie, the business diversified from drapery into other areas until it gradually became the very much enlarged and multi-faceted department store of today. Barker's of Northallerton still remains a family concern, with Leslie's youngest son Charles Barker today's managing director.

Fairburn's chemist's shop near to the Black Bull on the east side of Town Street (High Street), 1880s. The proprietor was Joseph Fairburn, who was a prominent citizen and a member of the Northallerton Masonic Anchor Lodge, and had owned the shop since 1868. Fairburn's remained as one of the main Northallerton chemists until after the Second World War and the family was especially well known for their musical talents.

John Boston had established a grocer's shop in Northallerton before 1850 between the Black Swan and the Three Tuns public houses on the east side of the High Street. By the time this photograph was taken at the turn of the century it was one of the main shops in town, and under the third generation of 'John Boston grocer' it prospered until the 1960s. This John Boston was born in 1883, and though his expertise was in the grocery trade he went into the property business with builder Arthur Smith; the partnership did much to aid the residential growth of the town between 1918 and 1939. The Boston business link is still present in the town as John's eldest daughter Dorothy married Leslie Barker.

Another well-established shop is pictured here – that of H. Rider, pork butcher, almost at Romanby Road on the west side of the High Street in about 1900. In those days Romanby Road corner opposite the Durham Ox was known as Rider's Corner, as another Rider's shop was there too, selling furniture. The enterprising Rider family took over Plews Brewery at Leeming Bar in the mid-1920s, and also created the Vale of Mowbray factory, which specialised in bacon and pork production. It had become a highly successful business of national repute by the time it was taken over in 1963.

T. Place and Sons' timber business, with a wood yard on the west side of North End near the railway crossing, was very successful. Early this century horse teams were used for traction and timber haulage, as seen here. It seems amazing that horses were the main means of haulage until after the First World War. Thomas Place, the founder of the firm, was a leading North Riding county councillor, being elected an alderman. He lived at Sowber Gate.

The Archer family came to Northallerton from Middlesbrough in 1920 to start a very successful haulage, removals, furniture, motor and engineering business. This Daimler van of the early 1920s had solid rubber tyres, belonged to Horace Archer and was used for furniture removal, whilst his brother Percy initially concentrated on low lorries and tippers for use by the town's builders, such as Stockdale and Oakley, before starting the motor garage on the edge of Bourne's field at the south end of South Parade (now Sanderson Ford Used Car Centre). The several branches of the business were eventually unified by Percy's son Brenny.

When the railway came to Northallerton in the 1840s there were two passenger stations at first – one on the present main line station site and the other at the North End, adjacent to the North Bridge and Willow Beck. The latter soon became the goods station and operated with an extensive goods yard and accompanying fleet of goods vehicles for well over a century. This photograph is of a presentation to motor drivers at the goods yard on 21 September 1960. Fronting the motor vehicle loaded with cattle feed are, left to right, R. Bell (goods agent), W. Ellis (driver), W. Megginson (porter), D. Wetherill (porter), D. Lee (driver), A. Metcalfe (driver), S. Fawcett (porter), M. Simpson (driver), R. Bell (goods agent), T. Wetherstone (driver), H. Richardson (foreman), A. Carlton (driver), W. Goodchild (shunter).

Alastair Carter, the son of Mr and Mrs Harry Carter of Castle Hills Farm, was one of the most talented and best-known people of his generation. He attended the Applegarth and National schools, went into the family business and led a very popular dance band, the Swingtimers, before the Second World War, during which he became a Royal Air Force officer and bomber pilot. After the war he became a councillor and the chairman of Northallerton UDC before moving to the Midlands to pursue his engineering business, Carter Engineering. Here Alistair produced an electric car, the Carter Coaster, with which he is seen on 25 October 1967 outside his factory at Tamworth. He could not get it mass produced in Britain, but took his invention to the USA; there it became widely used as a golf caddy car, and its success brought him invitations to the White House in Washington.

The welcoming staff of Nathaniel Russell's grocer's shop stand behind their counter in this animated and detailed study of the 1930s. This shop and adjacent café were amongst the foremost businesses in the town until their closure in the 1960s. They were situated on the west side of the High Street on the site now occupied by Mister Minit and Superdrug, and had been started in the nineteenth century by Nathaniel Russell's father of the same name. The gentlemen on the photograph are, left to right, Freddy Brown, Ken Hoyle and Mr Smith ('Smithy').

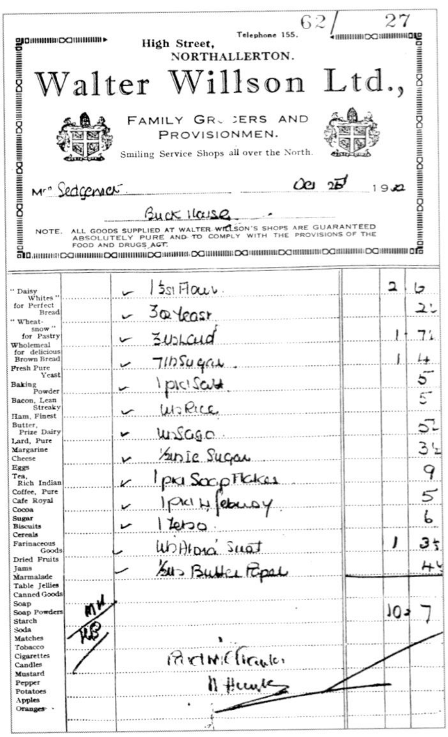

62/ 27

Telephone 155.

High Street,
NORTHALLERTON.

Walter Willson Ltd.,

FAMILY GR..ERS AND
PROVISIONMEN.

Smiling Service Shops all over the North.

Mrs Sedgewick Oct 25 1932

Brick House

NOTE. ALL GOODS SUPPLIED AT WALTER WILLSON'S SHOPS ARE GUARANTEED ABSOLUTELY PURE AND TO COMPLY WITH THE PROVISIONS OF THE FOOD AND DRUGS ACT.

"Daisy Whites" for Perfect Bread
"Wheat-snow" for Pastry
Wholemeal for delicious Brown Bread
Fresh Pure Yeast
Baking Powder
Bacon, Lean Streaky
Ham, Finest
Butter, Prize Dairy
Lard, Pure
Margarine
Cheese
Eggs
Tea, Rich Indian
Coffee, Pure
Cafe Royal
Cocoa
Sugar
Biscuits
Cereals
Farinaceous Goods
Dried Fruits
Jams
Marmalade
Table Jellies
Canned Goods
Soap
Soap Powders
Starch
Soda
Matches
Tobacco
Cigarettes
Candles
Mustard
Pepper
Potatoes
Apples
Oranges

	s	d
1½st Flour	2	6
3oz Yeast		2½
3lbs Lard	1	7½
7lbs Sugar	1	4
1pkt Salt		5
1lb Rice		5
1lb Sago		5½
½lb Ic Sugar		3½
1pkt Soap Flakes		9
1pkt H[illegible]		5
1 Zebo		6
1lb Atora Suet	1	3½
½lb Butter Paper		4½
	10	7

MH
RB

[illegible]
[illegible]

Although the cost of living and prices have soared, this grocery bill of 25 October 1932 amounting to 10 shillings and 7 pence from Walter Willson's for Mr Sedgwick of Brick House Farm, Darlington Road, will evoke nostalgic memories of shopping days far gone. Walter Willson's stood on the site now occupied by Betty's Café.

A relatively modern scene of the later 1950s, but one to jog memories. Mr Bateman (left), the proprietor of Thompson's butcher's shop, is hard at work preparing meat on the old familiar curved butcher's block, and David Carr is in the then standard butcher's overall. Thompson's of Northallerton is still on the south-east side of the High Street.

Clapham's shop was started in the 1880s by the enterprising John W. Clapham, but had progressed far by 1952 when Clapham's Fashion Show took place. Valerie Cappelman is seen here in the foreground modelling a dress. Clapham's merged with Upton's in 1963, and gave way to Boyes Store in 1977.

DiPalma's ice cream van has been a welcome sight to youngsters in the Northallerton district since the Second World War, and here in the 1950s is a typical scene at a show. Three DiPalma brothers, Tony, Thomas ('Mazzi') and Albert, brought the business to Northallerton from Bishop Auckland in the late 1930s, and DiPalmas still have a strong presence in the town and area.

Every business in the town has always been dependent for its success on its staff. This is the Boots the Chemist staff dinner at the Golden Lion in 1963. Left to right: Mavis Suttil, John McIntyre, Ellen Metcalfe, Marion Fowler, Annette Winn, Bob Birch (Manager), Charlotte Foxton, Dorothy Ashby, Veronica Binks, Barbara Wilson, Bob Turnbull.

CHAPTER SEVEN

MUSIC & ENTERTAINMENTS

Musicians, amateur entertainers, actresses, actors and artistes have added spice, colour and culture to life in Northallerton down the ages and have thrived in the twentieth century. Northallerton Operatic Society produced Patience *in 1919 outdoors at the Close, Brompton, where some of the cast pose. On the extreme right is Miriam Harrison and on the extreme left Mrs Yeoman Stead. Others in the cast were Ida Jones (née Sturgiss) and Bill Willan (a solicitor). Miriam Harrison, then aged sixteen, went on to sing professionally for D'Oyly Carte. She was trained by Mrs Annie Guthrie, married and called her daughter Patience. As Pat Mitchell, her daughter produced several Northallerton operatic and variety productions in the 1960s and 1970s.*

The South End Methodist church had a concert party called Lucky Numbers in the 1920s. Here is the cast of *The Arrival Esmirola*. Back row, left to right: Frank Hutchinson, Marjorie Espiner, Fred Morley. Middle row: Peggy Sykes, Cic Sturdy, Barbara Sykes. Front row: Ruth Thompson, Fred Archer.

The East Road National School staged concerts regularly in the interwar years. Its senior girls are photographed here a concert at the Zion church schoolroom in 1936. Left to right: Olga I'Anson, Nita Cornforth, Joan Derbyshire, Marjo Marshall, Joyce Parry, Miss Mallinson, Renee Wright, Miss Burton, Kathleen Stevens, Audrey Carr.

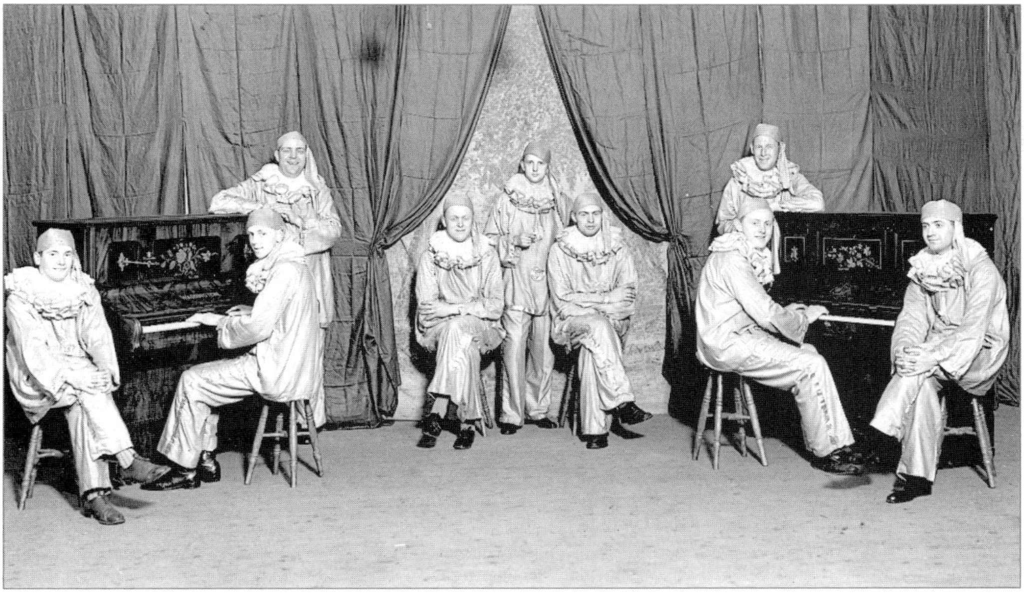

Northallerton's premier entertainment group in the 1930s was The Jolly Boys. Two of their stalwarts were 'Nobby' Clark (third left) and Johnny Rook (at the piano on the right).

In 1951, to celebrate the Festival of Britain, a pageant lasting three days was produced on 18, 20 and 23 June. It took as its theme the history of Northallerton, and involved 300 actors and actresses, cast by Mrs Harriet Lord, principal of Wensley House School on South Parade. Pictured is Hugh McMaster, who played the Scottish escort to Charles I in 1647. In reality, Hugh was the North Riding of Yorkshire educational architect.

Northallerton Amateur Operatic Society was revived after the Second World War and subsequently has staged large annual productions of a very high standard; these have given enormous pleasure to the Northallerton public. The ladies photographed here were amongst the main members in the 1950s. Back row, left to right: Margaret Umpleby, Grace Wilson, Joan Stevens, Mrs Bramley, Pat Pearson, Robina Pearson, Miss Hebden. Seated: -?-, Catherine Wilson, -?-, Christine Hodgson, Helen Wilson, Dorothy Young. Catherine Wilson went on to sing professionally for Scottish Opera, taking many soprano lead parts and gaining a fine national reputation.

Millie Messenger was the piano accompanist for Northallerton Operatic Society and Northallerton Variety Company for over four decades. Her first public performance was at the age of thirteen, when she entertained the troops at Northallerton Town Hall during the First World War; she accompanied the silent films at the Cinema de Lux in the 1920s; taught piano playing for sixty years; and when she had this photograph taken for *Showboat* in 1971 she still had twenty years of public appearances ahead of her. Millie recently celebrated her ninety-fifth birthday.

The Northallerton Operatic Society performed *The Student Prince* at the Lyric Cinema to packed houses for a week in November 1961. Pictured here are three of the principals, and stalwarts of the society. Left to right: Michael Wilson, Olwyn Evans and Tom Umpleby (seated). Michael's father, Tom Wilson (known as 'TG'), was the inspirational producer at the time, and the whole Wilson family featured prominently in the productions.

These young dancers were just embarking on their amateur operatic careers when they performed in *Showboat*, the Northallerton Operatic Society's production in November 1971. Pat Mitchell was the producer, Bob Barratt the musical director and the venue was the Allertonshire School (West). Left to right: Janet Smith, Julie Beckwith, Deborah Jones, Maureen Hartley, Pauline Wilson, Julie Harrison. Alison Parnaby is seated in front.

The Allertonshire Players has been the leading amateur dramatic group in Northallerton from the Second World War up to the present day, with a change of name to the Allerton Players in the 1970s. Some of their young actresses, such as Judy Bailey and Susan Bennett, have gone on to become professionals, and this society has achieved and maintained a very high standard of performance in its presentations – which have been produced annually for over fifty years. Here is the cast of *Jane Steps Out*, photographed at the Friarage Hospital's new nurses' recreation room in January 1958. Standing, left to right: Barry Cawthorne and Arthur Robson. Seated: Kath Bacon, Valerie Wilkinson, Kathleen McCartney, Mrs J.A. Bull, Joan Stevens. Barry and Joan were married soon afterwards.

Northallerton Grammar School also staged regular plays, especially in the 1950s when Edwin Bush, the history master, was the patient producer and Lloyd Dales of the Allertonshire Players would assist. The school, under the direction of Jimmy Addison, built a stage in the main school hall: here William Shakespeare's *Twelfth Night* was performed in March 1952. The cast is shown here. Standing, left to right: Pauline Thompson, Helen Dales, Dorothy Sunter, John Boynton, Catherine Wood, Mick Riordan, Brian Raine, John Severs. Front row: Vivienne Taylor and Paddy Earnshaw.

The Northallerton district has always boasted a good dance band to play at local occasions – for example, Alastair Carter's The Swingtimers, then Bert Sherwood's band and latterly The New Sound Five, led by Andrew Bramley. In the 1950s a most entertaining, skilled and popular dance band was that of Bert Langthorne of Brompton, who himself could play several musical instruments. Here is the band in 1955 at a Northallerton Town Hall Christmas Social giving the dancers a real kick! Left to right: Billy Grainger, Gordon Kitching, Charlie McCabe, Tommy Young and Bert Langthorne, at the piano.

Another totally different group, but also high quality, stylish and popular, was the Northallerton pipe band of the early 1960s, eventually called the Northallerton British Legion Pipe Band. They practised all over the town to improve their skills (at the Wesleyan schoolroom, the Lino factory, the Golden Lion, Brompton Linen Mill, Archers Castle Hills and finally the British Legion) and were in great demand, leading many parades in Northallerton and performing at shows in the surrounding villages. Back row, left to right: Pipe Major Jimmy Kay, Tommy Wilbor, Ronnie Wilbor, Joe Good, Angus Goodall, Ian MacQuaker. Front row: Ron Amer, Len Allison, Harry Thompson and Ray Weston. Mr Weston is now a Chelsea Pensioner, who sometimes returns to the town, when his scarlet tunic adds colour to occasions.

The Girls Friendly Society gave variety shows just after the war. Here they are on the Church House stage on one such occasion in 1949 after performing their various songs, dances and sketches. Back row, left to right: Eileen Burnett, Jean Dunlop, Maureen Hardisty, Jean Larder, -?-, Betty Freer, Joyce Render, Gwen Symons, Daphne Dobby, Mary Pearson, Betty Lewis, Bessie Dale, Sheena Wilson. Front row: Pam Swan, Jean Mason, Vina Galloway, Miss Hewson (behind Jean Tyler), Jean Tyler, Norah Bowes, -?-, Marjorie Gill, Audrey Wintersgill, Judith Mathison, Margaret Lancaster, Janice Hopps, Eileen Cullen, Christine Lightfoot, Jean Clarke, Jennifer Wilson, Brenda Robson, -?-.

Various organisations staged concerts in the 1950s, and here is the cast of the Zion Congregational Girls Guild at their concert in the Zion Schoolroom in 1952. Back row, left to right: Margaret Dunn, Sheila Wilbor, Pat Jackson, Isobel Sherwood, Barbara Wilson, -?-. Front row: Susan Riordan (author's youngest sister), Jean Carter, Rita Trufitt, -?-, ? Mattinson, -?-, Wilma Fawcett.

rthallerton Variety Company has given enormous pleasure to countless local people from the early 1950s to the sent day, with innumerable memorable productions. Significantly, they have given the profits of their efforts to many erent charities. Probably their highlight of every year has been the annual pantomime each January, which has been of rofessional standard, has brought folks flocking and, most of all, has made children hoarse and happy. In 1956 they ged *Cinderella*, with Lady Barwick as producer; as Valerie Ward she had been a film actress with such as James Mason Ralph Richardson. Many stalwarts of the Variety Company line up here. In the centre is Mary Weir (Cinderella) to left of Pat Mitchell (Prince Charming); between them is Terence Naylor (Buttons). Geoff Naylor (fifth right) and Cec hardson (third right) are the Ugly Sisters, with Ron Jones (the Baron) in between. Also included are Vina Galloway ırth left), Judy Swan (fifth left) and Mercy Barlow (second right).

onymous with the word music ally from the 1940s to the later 50s were the great friends Gerry lson and Clifford Walker. Clifford s a virtuoso violinist, who is seen e in mid-concerto in 1953. He ted his musical career in a quartet ich included John Barbirolli, ame lead violinist with the erpool Philharmonic Orchestra taught music at Ampleforth llege before coming to rthallerton. In the town he shared ny a musical triumph with Gerry lson, who conducted great musical rks while Clifford led the hestra.

Gerry Wilson, seen here at his beloved piano in 1953, was the son of a Cumberland miner and a self-taught musical genius. He came to Northallerton in 1939 as choirmaster of the parish church and remained to captivate the whole town with his musical talents and performances, and his unique character, personality and sense of humour. Under his baton Northallerton Choral Society soared to heights that even the most imaginative reporters of the local musical scene found it almost impossible to describe, especially when Handel's *Messiah* was performed – usually at Christmastide in the parish church with eminent guest artistes, and Clifford Walker leading the orchestra. Gerry was equally magnetic with the parish church choir and the Gerry Wilson Award was inaugurated in his memory to be given annually to the most deserving chorister. The early deaths of Clifford (1967) and Gerry (1968) were a great loss to the town.

CHAPTER EIGHT

FARMING YESTERDAY

Farming has been at the heart of Northallerton's existence from its very early Saxon beginnings. In the Domesday Book of 1086 the town was described as having sixty-six villeins (freemen) with thirty ploughs. Nowadays urban development has pushed the farming frontier further and further back, but only fifty years ago farms with arable land and animals were only a stone's throw from the High Street. Castle Hills Farm was one of these, and here in the 1930s the family are joining in the haymaking as was the custom in those unmechanised days. Young Grace Carter stands with grandad William Carter to the left, with to the right grandad William Hawroyd (Leeds), her father Harry Carter and Grandma Alice Hawroyd. Town buildings are visible in the background.

It seems almost unbelievable that these agricultural scenes are only a few decades away; to the older generation they so familiar and comfortably normal. The horse ploughing is being carried out in the 1930s at Thornton-le-Moor, one the many villages and innumerable farms near Northallerton. Although unknown, the men are absolutely representat of their local farming fellows engaged in their daily labour.

Stooking taking place at Cross Lanes Farm, Scruton, 1930s. Left to right: Tom Barker, Bill Hewison, Mrs Heslewo Harry Firby.

evocative rural haytime scene at R.A. Raine's farm, Entercommon, 1923. Left to right: George Proctor, George
ıe (son) on the hayrake, Jack Pratt at the haycock and Robert Raine (son) with the dog.

wance' time. Remarkably this scene full of fascinating detail – the grazing horse, the characters and the hats – is even
rer in time, the 1950s at William Lancaster's farm at Brompton.

That farming was hard is undeniable but with the weather that assailed the country in the winter of 1940 it became virtually impossible. Clara Carter is at Castle Hills Farm, Northallerton, amid icicles the like of which may never be seen in Northallerton again.

The tractor may have been gradually replacing the horse in 1949 but a rueful Geoff Husband wasn't impressed with modern mechanisation when he was snapped on his bogged-down tractor on snowy Rayfield's Farm, Danby Wiske.

Shorthorns have been a speciality of the Northallerton area for centuries; the Booth herd at Warlaby in the late eighteenth century immediately springs to mind. Herbert Langthorne is displaying this shorthorn bull, which weighed 1 ton, at his Crawford Grange farm near Brompton, just prior to the Second World War. Such striking animals are rare now, with artificial insemination increasingly the vogue.

John Willis of Newby Wiske, early 1960s. He has taken a trade stand at a poultry fair at the Royal Hall, Harrogate, to advertise his frozen turkeys. He was an early entrepreneur in this area, who was soon processing thousands of turkeys a week, and he gained a national reputation in this sphere. An example of his enterprise was that he bought RAF Thornaby's guardroom for £80 in 1960 and used it as his administrative offices at Newby Wiske. With him on his trade stand are, left to right, Maisie Willis (sister), Mrs Sarah May Willis (mother) and Marion Willis (sister-in-law).

Young Farmers' Clubs sprang up quickly in the 1940s. The North Riding of Yorkshire was in the forefront of this movement, and Northallerton Young Farmers' Club was very prominent. These clubs were tremendously important for inter-communication, the cross-fertilisation of ideas, the experimentation and advance of new farming methods and finally from a social viewpoint, as the vocation was scattered and isolated by nature of its business. As early as 1945 the Northallerton Young Farmers' Club won the Myton Trophy for stock judging. The team is shown here. Left to right: George Harwood, Bert Langthorne, Brian Ward, Eric Garnett.

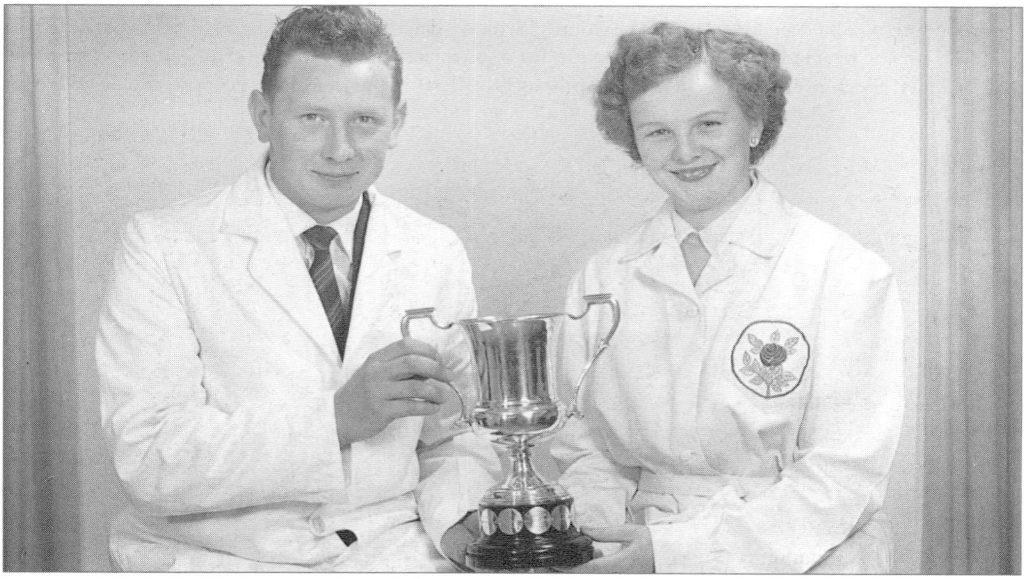

In the 1950s the Northallerton Young Farmers' Club was continuously successful in such competitions as the Darlington and Stockton Times public speaking contest for the North Riding, which it won at the Catholic church in Northallerton in March 1952. Several of its members were selected to go on foreign tours, such as Dick Willis (Sowber Hill) to New Zealand in 1950 and Bessie Metcalfe (Newby Wiske) to Canada in 1952. George Barker (Scruton) and Margaret Asquith (Bullamoor) are seen here in 1955 holding the trophy they have won as national champions of the Federation of Young Farmers' Clubs for poultry judging at the London Dairy Show, Olympia – a most notable achievement.

By 1955 the North Riding Federation of Young Farmers' Clubs had grown to 3,251 members and 43 clubs. Most of its activities were centred on Northallerton, mainly the Allertonshire School and the Town Hall, and district, such as Pasture House Farm (Mr and Mrs Leslie Barker) where the North Riding Annual Rally was held in June 1952. The Young Farmers' dances and balls were cheerful and animated, with the advice 'to stand back when they do the Lancers' springing to memory. Here is a Young Farmers' Ball at Northallerton Town Hall in 1952. In the centre, left to right: Robina Pearson, Pat Pearson and Nancy Wheatley, with faces visible, and John Willis, centre, facing them.

The Northallerton Young Farmers' Club social at Church House, 1955. George Barker is on the extreme back right, on the microphone, and next to him are Bert Langthorne and Mary Hauxwell. Others include Anne Taylor, Eddie Sherwood, Elizabeth Sherwood, Anne Sherwood, Greta Lightfoot, Phyllis Kirby, Marjorie Pearson, Doreen Tuer, Margaret Bosomworth, Alan Kirby, Ken Bradley, David Hill, Ralph Pattison, Chester and Robin Bosomworth.

The Bedale and Hurworth Hunt Farmers used to play each other in an annual cricket match, which was competitive but essentially friendly and sociable. In 1951 the match was played at Ingleby Cross; here the teams are mingled together for a photo-call. Back row, left to right: Jack Lowther (umpire), G. Brown (scorer), George Tate, -?-, Ross Simpson behind Ronnie Bratley, Bob Lowther, George Archibald, Bert Langthorne, Brian Clark, -?-, Spensley Raper (in cap), Peter Oldfield, Mr Bennett, Fred Bainbridge, Harry Brown, E. Greenwell, Mr Calvert, J. Darling, Edgar Smith (umpire). Front row: Teddy Kettlewell, John Shield, Roland Hill, John Pigg, Billy Prince, Peter Bell.

Definite signs that 'times are a-changing' are seen in this final farming reminiscence. The ABC TV outside broadcast cameras came to Pasture House Farm near Northallerton (belonging to Leslie and Dorothy Barker) on Sunday 27 December 1959. A live programme about Christmas on the farm was televised, and shown from 12.05 to 1.20 p.m. as part of 'The Other Man's Farm' series. Seen in action are the Loftus Sword Dancers. Many farming friends and also farmers who had appeared previously in the series attended what ABC Television termed 'a Christmas festival'. A good time was had by all. As live television was in its comparative infancy and as the broadcast concerned a well-known Northallerton family, great local interest was aroused.

CHAPTER NINE

SCHOOLDAYS

A most poignant and moving occasion is recorded here. Northallerton Grammar School's memorial to its old boys who died in the Second World War was dedicated by the Archbishop of York, Dr Cyril Garbutt, on 31 October 1949. It consisted of wrought-iron gates set into rustic brick pillars at the end of the northern and southern drives, with the latter bearing a bronze plaque inscribed with the names of the twenty fallen; on the photograph it is draped with a Union Jack. The Archbishop of York conducted the service, which included the deeply emotional hymn 'Oh Valiant Hearts', and the lesson was appropriately read by a fellow scholar of the dead Arnold Pearson DSO, DFC.

The clergy are, left to right, Canon Crawford, the Vicar of Crakehall, the Rev. F.T. Baines Vicar of Northallerton, and the Archbishop of York. The headmaster A.T. Richardson, is on the extreme left, Hazel Brown, the head girl, is to his right, and Miss Laura Webster and Arthur Arrand are on either side and behind Canon Crawford.

A sword dance during the National School concert at the Zion schoolroom, April 1936. Left to right: Marjorie Marshall, ? Burton, Olga I'Anson, Rita Riordan (the author's eldest sister), Marjorie Holmes, Joyce Hall.

Thirty two netball players in the National School yard, 1939. The teacher is Doris Brown, who soon afterwards became art mistress at the newly opened Allertonshire School. Back row, left to right: Connie Tweddle, Mary Johnson, Audrey Joyce, Muriel Glover, Nora Bowe, Doreen Blair, Joan Coates, Betty Carter, Miss Brown, Joyce Johnson, Joyce Hartley, Lulu Smith, Mary Foster, Florence Bowman. Middle row: Connie Richards, Doreen King, Elma Weighell, Doreen Gladwin, Grace Carter, Freda Fishburn, Jean Cowen, Eva Addison, Muriel Sollitt, Doreen Thompson. Front row: -?-, Joan Simons, Dorothy Gill, Sylvia Brown, Connie Brown, Margaret Hutchinson, Nellie Smith, Ivy Hall, Nancy Hutchinson.

Mr Alf Gunn's class is posing in the National School yard, with the Northallerton Workhouse as a backdrop, 1939. Back row, left to right: Billy Bell, Peter Ward, Maurice Wilshere, Peter Norman, Douglas Peacock, Alf Braithwaite, Desmond Wardle, Ken Turner, Derek Brown, Leslie Lyall, Billy Grainger, George Hepplestone, Henry Place, Frank Asquith. Second row: Alfie Whildon, Billy Trenholme, Billy Rutherford, John Walker, Lawrence Collins. Third row: Pat Dodsworth, Joan Robinson, Edna Berry, Audrey Joyce, Ruth Eyre, Dorothy Thompson, Doreen Wilbor, Edith Stockdale, Pat Trueman, Renee Brough and Raymond Freer. Front row: Dorothy Dobson, Grace Carter, Freda Fishburn, Joyce Chapman, Norma Longstaff, Joan Wilbor, Mary Johnson, Joan Green, Ruby Sawdon.

Miss Plummer's class, East Road National School, 1943. The play was *The Prince and the Cooking Pot*. Standing, left to right: Paddy Burcham, Derick Robinson, Cynthia Davidson, Jane Groves, Marjorie Martin, Betty Mitten, Elsie Coxall. Seated: Peter Wadsworth, Tony Palliser.

This Northallerton Grammar School hockey team was unbeaten in the 1947/8 season. The green and white sashes denote school colour holders. Standing, left to right: Miss Doris Dixon, Jean Ellwood, Peggy Peacock, Doris Crooks, Hazel Bellwood, Pam Hutchinson, Catherine Staples, Brenda Dale. Seated: -?-, -?-, Hazel Brown, Betty Atkins, Margot Garlick. Grammar School Lane is behind.

Walter Raine and Hazel Brown, Wensley House captains, receive the house champions' cup on sports day at Northallerton Grammar School, 1948. The headmaster A.T. Richardson looks on with French teacher Arthur Arrand (half hidden). Pupils, top row, left to right: Joan Almond, Margaret Thompson, Louie Coates (above), Christine Hodgson, Beryl Todd, Renee Knight. Front row: Ray Thomas, Valerie Cappleman, Jean Clarke, Valerie Wilkinson. Sports day was one of the highlights of the school year, with many visitors.

Northallerton Grammar School football team, 1948. Back row, left to right: Mick Riordan, N. Parkinson, J. Jameson, Roger Hartley, Harry Brown, Lew Randall. Front row: John Atkinson, Sean Crawford, Walter Raine, Derek Smales, Bill Roden.

rthallerton Grammar School boys PT display team in the gymnasium, 1949. They performed for speech day at the Lyric ema. Left to right: Vernon Tennant, Brian Glasper, Bill Roden, David Johnson, Bob Bennison on the shoulders of Peter sbeck, Derek Smales, Michael Wallace, Peter Fisher, George Barker.

Northallerton had the most consistently successful school cricket side in the area from 1948 to 1952. This is the 1948 team. Back row, left to right: Sean Crawford, Geoff Milburn, Tom Mace, -?-, Eric Boddye, Harold Young, Michael Wallace (scorer). Middle row: John Atkinson, Brian Colley, Derek Fowler, Alan Bennett, Walter Raine. Front row: Mick Riordan, Harry Brown.

The annual boys' cross country race was always run in March at Northallerton Grammar School, down Crosby Road and over the fields to the 'Targets' on Bullamoor and back. It was another red letter day in the year, watched by many spectators and every boy in the senior school (fourteen years old upwards) had to run, no excuses accepted! Here, in March 1948, the race has just started and the boys are sprinting down Grammar School Lane past the school. In front, left to right: Bob Bennison, George Barker, Derek Smales, Peter Raisbeck, John Atkinson.

action photograph of the junior boys' 220 yard race at Northallerton Grammar School's sports day in 1952, taken by off Todd. Not only does it include various members of the school at the time, but it is also an invaluable record of the thern aspect of the school, for soon afterwards this sports/cricket field was built upon. The runners are, left to right, stair Campbell, Geoff Brown, the taller David Severs and Eric Reed; recognisable amongst the spectators are Minnie , Marion Cowper, Joyce Kirtley, Will Grainger, John Gibson, John Cousins, Robert McKenzie, Stewart Walker, Mary nsden, Ian Blythe and Mollie Thompson. The view was unimpeded from Grammar School Lane round to Crosby Road Northallerton Gaol, showing the southern-facing window that had almost been bricked up following the March 1946 :. The walls are lower than today and indeed the prison, which is one of the oldest in use nationally, dates back to 1785 en it was erected as a house of correction by the North Riding of Yorkshire, along with a court house (then called the sions house), a prisoner governor's dwelling and an extension to the registry house which had already been sited vn Zetland Street in 1736. This cluster of North Riding county buildings, designed by the famous architect John r from 1783 to 1785, established Northallerton as the county town of the North Riding and is therefore of major torical importance.

Also of great interest are the farm buildings that can be seen at the bottom of the field. These date back to when this s the Golden Lion field in the eighteenth and nineteenth centuries in the heyday of the colourful stagecoach era before railway came to Northallerton in March 1841. Situated on the old Great North Road in the middle of Northallerton gh Street, the Golden Lion was a major staging hotel between London and Edinburgh, with a dozen coaches such as the legraph', 'Queen Charlotte' and 'Wellington' stopping daily. It had stabling at the rear for over thirty horses and they re rested and refreshed from their stagecoach labours in this very field. The latter was also bestowed a great accolade in 40 when it was chosen as the venue for the third ever Yorkshire Show, to which people came from far and wide. As the d has now been lost to modern building development this photograph, though initially of the Northallerton Grammar ool sports day, now takes on a much wider significance as a record of Northallerton's past.

Allertonshire Secondary Modern School opened in September 1941 and became a showpiece school, as it was one of the three first secondary modern schools in the country. Interested educationalists visited from home and abroad and a cine film was made of its activities. The children from the National and village schools, with a one teacher and one classroom environment, now had a varied secondary education in spacious buildings and surroundings. It was a revolution in schooling and added an enormous dimension to Northallerton and district's children's education and lives. It was the brainchild of the secretary of education of the North Riding, Frank Barraclough of Thirsk Road, Northallerton, and was the flagship of an enormous North Riding building programme that involved over fifty new schools and major extensions. This is class 3A with their teacher Miss Halliday and many happy smiles in 1950. Back row, left to right: Kenneth Coates, Derek Parkin, Clifford Bloomfield, Donald Farndale, Geoffrey Garnett, William Hutchinson, Reginald Thompson, John Charlton, William Bowes, Kenneth Robson, Lewis Lancaster, John Pollit. Third row: Moira Weighell, Anne Kendrew, Margaret Harker, Monica Martin, Dorothy Wilde, Margaret Foster, Diana Kirby, Jean Mason, Phyllida Warren, Jean Larder, Edna Carr, Margaret Kilvington. Second row: Sheila Robinson, Shirley Cussons. Pauline Henry, Shirley Reid, Miss Holliday, Gladys Watson, Norma Hargreaves, Margaret Gaines, Joan Stockdale. Front row: Margaret Moody, Patricia Mayes, Joan Hall, Veronica Kirby.

The Allertonshire prefects with the headmaster, Norman Bryning, 1950. Back row, left to right: Jean Ford, Roy Moody, Eileen Taylor, John Telford, Tony MacLean, Jeanette Middlemiss, Lorna Ware, Helen Dennis. Front row: Eileen Burnett, David Bramley, Dorothy Kendrew, Peter Natrass, Mr Norman Bryning, Anne Kirby, Gary Trousdale, Shirley Peacock, Anthony Hood.

om its earliest days Allertonshire School encouraged and excelled at sports. Cricket was a forte and the school soon oduced Doug Burnett, who played for Yorkshire 2 XI, and Arthur 'Rocker' Robinson from Brompton, who won his county cap playing for Yorkshire in the county championship for several years. Here is the 1950 team from which n Palmer went on to captain Northallerton CC 1 XI. Back row, left to right: Ernest Taylor (master), Alex Jackson, y Moody, Terry McLean, Brian Ward, Gary Trousdale, -?-, -?-, John Weatherill, Norman Bryning (headmaster). ated: Malcolm Cardino, Reg Porter, Peter Nattress, Michael Sturgiss, John Palmer, -?-, Richard Boddye. Norman yning was headmaster from 1945 to 1964, and gave the new school great stability.

lertonshire School soon began to oduce regular plays and concerts its magnificent new hall with a rpose-built stage. This is a scene om *Henry VIII*, produced in 1949, th Geoff Husband (Henry VIII), ne Hardcastle (Anne Boleyn) and ymond Calvert (page boy).

Allertonshire School also excelled at football, under Stan Schofield, the sports master, who had been a gifted cen forward and remained at the school encouraging all sports for many years. The team of 1950/1 lines up here. Back ro left to right: Roy Moody, Brian Ward, David Bramley, Peter Nattrass, Tony McLean, David Hollingworth, David Pears Front row: Stan Schofield (sports master), Billy Hutchinson, David Kendrew, John Metcalfe, Harry Wilbor, Tony Graing Norman Bryning (headmaster).

The Parents and Staff Association has always been most active and supportive at Allertonshire School, and in 1950 t parents played the school at cricket. Back row, left to right: Gary Trousdale, -?-, -?-, Mr Pratt, -?-, Ken Palmer, Ge Blair, Harry ('Joe') Render, Richard Boddye, -?-, -?-, John Hartley, -?-, Norman Read, Alex Jackson (scorer). Front ro Roy Moody, Peter Nattrass, John Palmer, Reg Porter, Michael Sturgiss, Brian Ward, Michael Cardino, -?-, -?-.

With the sweeping educational changes of the 1940s all the pupils at East Road National School now either went to Northallerton Grammar School or the Allertonshire Schools when they were eleven until they were fifteen (later sixteen). A happy East Road School Class 3 (aged ten to eleven) face the camera with their teacher Miss Tweedy in 1951. Back row, left to right: Robert Gibson, John Parsley, -?-, Christopher Todd, Peter Newton, John Wake, -?-, Robin Sanderson, Richard Robinson, Cambell Davidson, Robin Hardy-King, Robert Gladwin. Third row: David Rae, Elsie Chapman, Gwen Parker, Barbara Nelson, Margaret Dalton, Geraldine Dundas, Jean Bellwood, Sheila Middleton, Pauline Dawson, Ann Catchpole, Peter Walker. Second row: Mavis Hutchinson, Susan Riordan (author's youngest sister), Margaret Walker, Daphne Grimley, Maureen Gates, Miss Tweedy, Olive Nixon, Audrey Taylor, Ann Pashby, Celia Fawcett, Peggy Adams. Front row: Leonard Larder, David Morritt, William Flatters, David Tyreman, Keith Mason, Henry Hall, -?-, Alan Abbott, Harry Millar, -?-.

East Road School classes were still smiling when Mrs Bent's class of nine- to ten-year-olds was photographed in the school yard, 1960. The school closed in 1980, bringing 137 years of schooling to an end, and the building is now used by North Yorkshire Social Services. Back row, left to right: Richard Brown, Gary O'Neal, Michael Halliday, David Tyler, Philip How, Michael Kelly, Peter Swan, Donald Jack, Norman Allison, Michael McCready, Michael Evitt. Second row: David Wilkinson, Colin Straw, Ronnie Dorlin, Barbara Ward, Jean Scales, Susan Ramsey, Cathleen Graham, Cynthia Cocks, David Charlesworth, Michael Codd, Anthony Jones, Andrew Sedgwick. Front row: Angela Trees, Rita Pollard, Linda Grey, Elizabeth Grainger, Susan Jones, Trudy Holstead, Cathleen Hodgson, Valerie Pullan, Diana Richardson, Jane Armour, Kathleen Carr.

Northallerton Grammar School football team had their best season for a decade in 1951/2 and are seen here in March 1952. Back row, left to right: John Severs, Walter Hall, Dick Harris, Donald Richardson, Peter Grainger, Keith Hall, Billy Haynes. Front row: John DiPalma, David Simpson, Mick Riordan, Brian Glasper, Roger Hartley, Ronnie Holden.

These girls in the fourth year at Northallerton Grammar School in summer 1949 were among those who passed the first 11-plus examination in 1945, gaining free places at the school. Back row, left to right: Sheena Wilson, -?-, Jean Shepherd, Christine Hodgson, Mary Squince, Margaret Neesham, June Fowler. Front row: Barbara Dunning, Kathleen Hutchinson, Rhoda Chapman, Jean Dunlop, Brenda Dale.

The girls of Northallerton Grammar School had a fine sporting record at hockey, tennis and athletics, producing many North Riding county representatives in the 1950s. Here is the excellent school hockey team of 1953, containing five North Riding county players. Back row, left to right: Ruth Metcalfe, Valerie Wilkinson, Helen Dales, Jill Clarkson, Janette Goonan, Jill Harrison. Front row: Brenda Hartley, Irma Pattison, Marjorie Thompson, Catherine Wood, Jessie Ayling, Louie Coates.

Northallerton Grammar School tennis team, 1953. Back row, left to right: Louie Coates, Jean Clarke, Dorothy Garlick, Valerie Wilkinson. Front row: Marjorie Thompson, Helen Dales, Brenda Hartley.

This Northallerton Grammar School class of 1948 is 3B, under the tutelage of George Gardner, the popular scie master. Back row, left to right: Doug Metcalfe, Colin Parkinson, Willy Simpson, Bryan Foster, Ernold Cuthbert. Secc row: Alan Brown, John Gibson, John Scott, Jeff Lancaster, Barry Kettlewell, John Sheehan, Peter Vickerton, W Grainger. Front row: Joyce Wheldon, Lucy Marwood, Anne Megson, Pauline Watson, Jessie Ayling, Joan Welford, R Knight, Eileen Appleton. The class size of twenty-one is around the average size number of all the Grammar Sch classes at this date.

Northallerton Grammar School inner quadrangle is little changed since 1951 except for the disappearance of the bicyc now replaced by motor cars! This group of fourth form girls appears to be advertising school milk as a must for you ladies. Back row, left to right: Janette Goonan and Jean Clarke. Front row: Josephine Douglas, Joy Simpson, Vale Cappleman, Dorothy Bainbridge.

Northallerton Grammar School 4A in 1951, with their form master Jimmy Addison, the well-known woodwork teacher who was at the school for many years. Back row, left to right: John Severs, Robert Wilson, Walter Lonsdale, Keith Hall, John Dunning, Neil Arnott, Graham Nicholls. Second row: Jane Allinson, Enid Taylor, -?-, Minnie Lee, Joy Simpson, Valerie Cappleman, Janette Goonan, Raymond Peacock, Ivy Singleton, Dorothy Auton. Front row: Joyce Kirtley, Jean Clarke, Jimmy Addison, Dorothy Bainbridge, Pat Hutton, Audrey Fall.

By sports day in 1954 cricket and athletics had moved over to the new sports field at the south of the school, because building had reduced the area of the traditional sports field on the northern side. Colstan Road is in the background. A keen tussle over the junior hurdles is taking place. Left to right: Joyce Whitfield, Joan Phizacklea, Gillian Storm, Dorothy Thompson.

As a finale to the Schooldays chapter, here are the oldest and newest photographs of the selection. Northallerton Grammar School Scout Troop are seen here at Scout Camp at Runswick Bay in 1937. Standing, left to right: Alan Ward, George Law, Geoff Lyall, -?-, Peter Willoughby, -?-, -?-, Alan Mathison, John Randall, Brian Hill. Seated: Gus Clarke, -?-, -?-, Desmond Hill, -?-, Leonard Hodgson, Peter Ward, -?-. Very soon afterwards several enlisted in the RAF and sadly some were killed on active service – including George Law and Alan Mathison.

In 1961 East Road School won the Northallerton Primary Schools Football Cup, competing against Applegarth, Romanby and Brompton primary schools. The boys did not receive individual trophies but they did get a bar of chocolate and sixpence each! Left to right: Trevor Grainger, Cliff Jack, Dave Gilbank, Mike Cox, Ray Wilbor, Dave Codd, Tim Wilson, Ken Young, Steve Salt, Phil Wayman, Mike Bickerton.

CHAPTER TEN

OCCASIONS & EVENTS

Northallerton has been a vital link on the main London to Edinburgh railway line since the opening of the Great North of England Railway between Darlington and York on 30 March 1841. This excellent communication system consolidated the town's position as the county town of the North Riding of Yorkshire. The scene here is of a major engineering operation to construct a railway bridge on the low level loop line, under the main railway line just south of Northallerton railway station at Broomfield, in 1931. Numerous men were employed and the feat was carried out within twenty-four hours without stopping the rail traffic on the main line – a major achievement. Northallerton railway station is seen to the north with the main line running directly through. At that time it had five platforms (three north-bound for the main and Wensleydale lines and two south-bound for the main and Leeds lines) and three branch lines (Wensleydale, Hartlepool/Middlesbrough and Leeds). The busy station complex included a popular restaurant and a W.H. Smith's bookstall.

Since the war memorial in the south-eastern corner of Northallerton churchyard was dedicated on 6 August 1921 an Armistice Day parade and service have taken place here annually. Here the occasion is seen in 1955: the various wreath-laying contingents are lined up along the edge of the main road, with the Royal Air Force Association standard bearer Harold Bartram in the foreground and the Vicar, the Revd Stephen S. Thistlewood conducting the solemn Remembrance service. At the most poignant moment, the two minutes' silence in memory of the fallen, the town is completely stilled and silent.

In 1937 the Northallerton Army Cadets (Green Howards) contingent won the North Riding Cadet Forces small arms shooting competition, and they group around their trophy in their headquarters, the Drill Hall, Thirsk Road. They proudly wear the Green Howards cap badge which many of them and other local men were to do in the Second World War. Standing at the back: Instructor Trimmer. Middle row, left to right: George Kelley, Keith Beilby, John Carter, Robert ('Bob') Pattison, Keith Sherwood. Front row: Ray Johnstone, Wilf Cousins.

The dedication of the Green Howards Association Northallerton Branch Standard took place at the parish church on Sunday 25 August 1957. The Northallerton contingent is just passing down the High Street with the new Standard held in front by their chairman, Tom Riordan MBE (the author's father). The Green Howards regiment was granted the Freedom of Northallerton in 1980, and appropriately George Kelley (see p. 86), an ex-Green Howard, was Mayor of Northallerton when the entire First Battalion Green Howards paraded under their CO, Lieutenant-Colonel John Byrne.

The Freedom of Northallerton was conferred upon RAF Leeming in 1978, and the station's close rapport with the town is illustrated here in 1955. The film *The Dam Busters* was showing at the Lyric Cinema and, to mark the occasion and the RAF–Northallerton links, a reception was held at the cinema for RAF Leeming, the local Royal Air Force Association and Northallerton Urban District Council officials. Left to right: members of the RAF Escort, Mrs Innes-Crump, Sir Richard Barwick, Lady Barwick (film star Valerie Ward), Colonel Sir Charles Fitton, Cliff Colwell and Denis Beadle (Royal Air Force Association), Group Captain J.E. Innes-Crump (CO, RAF Leeming), Ritchie C. Pick (chairman of Northallerton UDC), Gladys Pick, Lady Fitton.

On August Bank Holiday Monday 1956 the first beauty competition was held in Northallerton since before the Second World War; over three thousand people attended out of a population of just over six thousand. The extent of the crowd is seen from this photograph, taken from Northallerton Grammar School roof, of the sports field where the event was staged. The winner was Anne Pegden, aged twenty. There were forty entrants for the event, which was part of a field day to raise money for the Northallerton War Memorial Baths Fund. Nora Swinburn (film and TV actress) and Lady Barwick were two of the judges.

Mercy Barlow became Miss Northallerton in 1959 in the event's fourth and last year, and is seen here holding the trophies. The Grammar School was still the venue and an equally large crowd of spectators attended as before. Some of the judges on this occasion were Paul Massey, the Canadian film star, Yvonne Buckingham, a 'film starlet', and Anthony Asquith, the famous film director who had made the nostalgic war-time film *The Way to the Stars* in 1944. It had been located at Catterick and was filmed in and around Northallerton, including at the Golden Lion.

This is the chorus of the Northallerton Variety Company's production of the pantomime *Cinderella* in January 1956. Left to right: Janet Pegden, Vina Galloway, Jean Pearson, Margaret Kilvington, Judy Swan, Anne Pegden, Pauline Watson, Mercy Barlow and Jean Utley. Anne, Vina and Mercy were all Miss Northallerton, in 1956, 1958 and 1959 respectively.

Before and after the Second World War garden parties were very much in vogue, and this one was held at the home of Mr and Mrs George Hird, Highfield in Thirsk Road, for the Zion Congregational church. The Hirds were one of the best-known Northallerton families, with George Hird a leading chemist with a shop in the High Street, a JP and chairman of Northallerton Cricket Club. How times have changed: the garden and tennis court have been built upon to accommodate Southwoods Residential Nursing Home.

National Safety Week in 1950 culminated with a procession through the High Street. Here members of Northallerton Fire Brigade are simulating the olden days when the tender was manually pulled to a fire when horse power failed. Left to right: Bert Cowton, Les Myers, Jack Longstaff, Norman Weatherill; Allertonshire schoolgirl Joyce Render is with her bicycle on the right. The picture is also a good depiction of the east side of the High Street, with the Registry House trees, Miss Lee's cake shop, Lloyds Bank and Mayford House (the white building) seen left to right.

The Wolf Cubs and Northallerton Grammar School Company of Girl Guides pass the parish church on the St George's Day parade, 1954. A large crowd presses forward on the left. Scouter George Hepplestone is saluting, while the first four in the outside line of the Guides, from the front, are Doreen Smith, Dorothy Thompson, Jennifer Bensley, Lana Cockerill.

Angela Norwood, aged sixteen, receives the Queen's Guide Citation and Badge in 1963 from the North Riding county commissioner Mrs Marshall, with, to the right, Mrs Muriel Hird, district commissioner and Mrs R. Wotherspoon, divisional commissioner. Angela attended Northallerton Grammar School and was the daughter of Mr and Mrs N. Norwood of Railway View, Northallerton. She had been in the Brownies since she was seven and was a patrol leader of the 1st Northallerton Guide Company.

As the country's telephone system went on to STD Northallerton's manually operated telephone exchange was phased out. The last GPO operators' shift is in progress here in September 1973 at the Northallerton Telephone Exchange, and considering the job situation the three ladies look very cheerful! Left to right: Marion Norwood, Dorothy Welton, Hilda Tyres.

These festive dancers were at the Town Hall Boxing night dance in 1938. The Swingtimers' Dance Band was led by Alastair Carter, with Harry Fairburn, Harry Wetherill and Max Errey providing the toe-tapping music. This band was very popular, as were Town Hall dances, which were held regularly on Saturday nights until the 1960s.

A Northallerton Rotary Club ball at the Golden Lion, mid-1950s. Back row, left to right: Michael Wilson (chairman, Northallerton UDC), G.H. Pulfrey (Rotary district chairman), Charles Sawdon (Northallerton Rotary chairman), S. Kirby (Northallerton Rotary vice-chairman), K. Bennifer (Northallerton Rotary secretary). Seated: Mrs Grace Wilson, Mrs Pulfrey, Mrs Lillian Sawdon, Mrs Kirby.

Northallerton Amateur Operatic Society's dance in November 1956 was held at the Golden Lion after their successful production of *Iolanthe*. Standing, left to right: Ronald Moffatt, June Parker, Len Bennett, Tom Umpleby, Barbara Cranston, Wallace Fairburn. Seated: Kathleen McCartney, Phyllis Elliot, John Common, Joan Stevens, Angela Wilson.

A vintage car rally was held at Northallerton annually from 1950 until the 1960s. At its height it was always started by the chairman of Northallerton UDC, and normally about thirty vintage cars ventured to Bedale and back. Here in the mid-1950s two of the most original engineers ever produced by Northallerton are enjoying the day – Wallace Weighell at the wheel with co-driver Alastair Carter.

The floods of 1931, caused when Sun Beck and Willow Beck burst their banks, have encroached on to the May Fair – but intrepid fairgoers are still braving the weather up and down the High Street. Flooding was quite regular with Sun Beck running down Bullamoor Road and beside Friarage Street. The Central Cinema House stands where the entrance to the Applegarth car park is today.

Better weather for the May Fair in 1955, with Crow's coronation waltzer prominent and people crowding on each side of the road. This 'play fair' dates by royal charter from 1610, although it may be several centuries older. As such it is one of the town's oldest traditions as well as the most popular, to which youngsters have resorted for many centuries. It is interesting to note cars travelling freely through the fair, whereas today the road is blocked off from Zetland Street to below the Town Hall.

early a year after the First World War ended on November 1918 a peace celebrations dinner for ex-rvicemen was held in the Town Hall. Here is a copy of e invitation to William Gamble, a county hall official, 10 was a volunteer and was wounded with the Green owards 4th Battalion at Ypres in 1915. John Hutton of lberge Hall, chairman of North Riding County Council r twenty years, proposed the main toast to 'fallen mrades'. It was a poignant night.

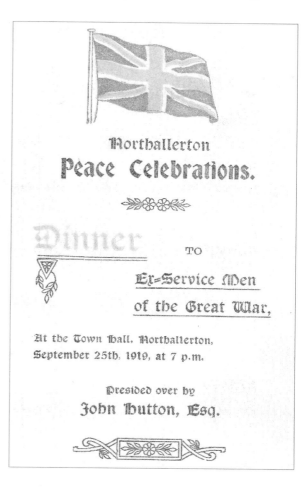

Northallerton

Peace Celebrations.

Dinner TO

Ex-Service Men

of the Great War,

At the Town Hall, Northallerton,
September 25th, 1919, at 7 p.m.

Presided over by

John Hutton, Esq.

Saturday, 14th December, 1940

A SPITFIRE DISPLAY

Over the Township of Northallerton and Romanby

at approximately 2-30 p.m.

SPITFIRE FLAG DAY

In the event of the Spitfire Display being cancelled owing to unfavourable weather, arrangements will be made for it to be given on the following Wednesday, the 18th December, 1940 when a Spitfire Flag Day will be held.

MAY WE APPEAL TO YOU TO MAKE YOUR TRIBUTE BY GIVING GENEROUSLY

Come into town and give the efforts your support.

Eric H. Smithson, Printer & Stationer, Northallerton.

Part of a war effort to buy a Spitfire in December 1940 is depicted by this notice. A Spitfire display took place over the town, a shot-down Messerschmitt 109 was on show behind the Urban District Council offices and over £5,000 was raised in Northallerton. Ironically a Spitfire crashed near Stone Cross only a short time later, in July 1941, and the pilot was killed.

Allertonshire School was opened during the Second World War in 1941. It was a showpiece school with a constant stream of visitors from Britain and foreign countries. This photograph of the school governors was taken at one of its very earliest speech days, Wednesday 7 May 1947. Left to right: George Hird, Councillor G East, Norman Bryning (headmaster), -?-, the Rev. Frederick Baines, Vicar of Northallerton, -?-. Norman Bryning celebrated his ninety-eighth birthday in 1998. He is a regular churchgoer, played golf until he was over ninety and is still an alert mine of information about past Northallerton and its people.

The High Street, which has witnessed centuries of events, is appropriately the last scene in this chapter The old shops of Porter (jewellers and opticians) and Russells (grocers and café) are prominent. The occasion is the dedication of the Bedale Northallerton Royal Air Forces Association Standard in 1955. It is being paraded past the saluting base, carried by Standard Bearer Harold Bartram. Front rank, left to right: Denis Beadle, Geoff Weatherill, Bill Smith. The salute was taken by the Commanding Officer of RAF Leeming, Group Captain J.E. Innes-Crump, with A.T. Richardson OBE, a wartime Group Captain and headmaster of Northallerton Grammar School, on his left and Roy Moody, chairman of Northallerton Urban District Council, on his right.

Chapter Eleven

A Sporting Town

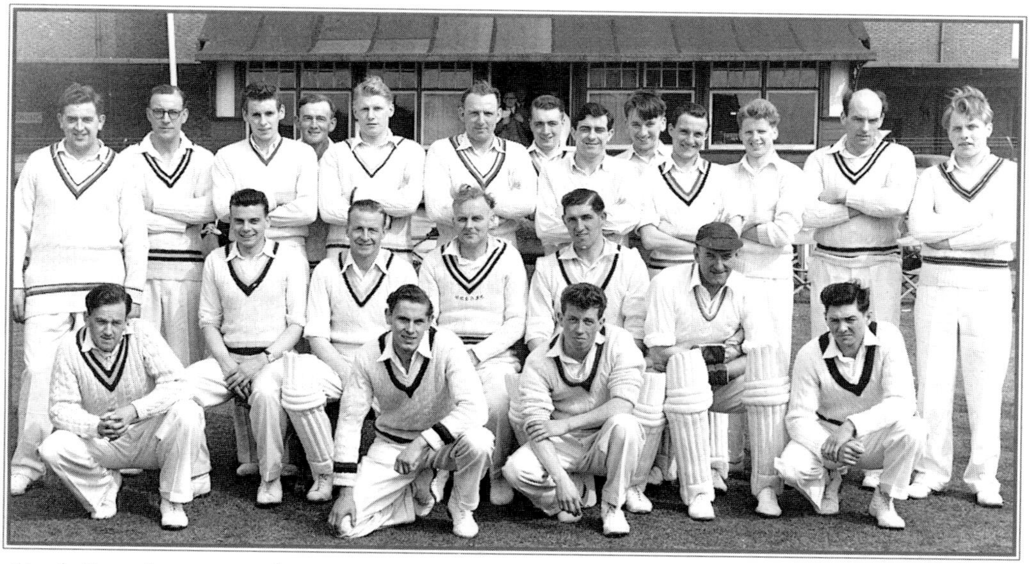

Northallerton's sporting pedigree is impressive, and goes back to the longbow. Among modern sports cricket is one of the oldest, with a game recorded in 1811 when the gentlemen of Northallerton were beaten by those of Danby Wiske by several 'notches'! All England played here in 1870, a full Yorkshire County team in 1903, 1904 and 1905 and Yorkshire returned to play in the 1950s and 1960s. These are the players that drew in the Yorkshire v. Northallerton match on Saturday 21 April 1956, including household names such as Fred Trueman and Dickie Bird. Back row, left to right: Mick Cowan (Yorks), Ron Diggle (Northallerton), Richard Clapham (Northallerton – Bedale), Brian Flintoff (Northallerton – Sessay) G. Booth (Yorks), Ron Appleyard (Yorks), Brian Bainbridge (Northallerton – Saltburn), Fred Trueman (Yorks), Ken Jones (Northallerton), Brian Bolus (Yorks), Terry McCabe (Northallerton – Thornaby), Eddie Oversby (Northallerton – Ripon), Doug Metcalfe (Northallerton). Second row: Dickie Bird (Yorks), Willie Watson (Yorks), Bill Pedley (Northallerton), Vic Wilson (Yorks), Denis Cooper (Northallerton). Front row: John Camburn (Northallerton – Darlington), Slingsby (Yorks), R Handley (Yorks), Jimmy Binks (Yorks). The score was Yorkshire 218 for 7 declared and Northallerton 64 for 8 (Trueman 3 for 16).

The Northallerton XI which played the Yorkshire 2nd XI, 1955. Back row, left to right: Ken Palmer (Umpire), Alan Pearson, Doug Metcalfe, Ken Jones, Ron Diggle, Don Pringle (Thirsk), Harry Brown, Albert Gaskell (who went on to umpire in the County Championship). Front row: Mick Riordan, John Broadley, Bill Pedley, Denis Cooper, John Camburn (Darlington).

A large crowd came to see the match between Northallerton and Middlesbrough Football Club in 1962. Several famous footballers were playing – including the renowned Brian Clough. The players mingled for the photograph. Back row, left to right: Harold Bartram (Northallerton), George Darwin (Northallerton), -?-, Peter Taylor (Middlesbrough), -?-, Alan Peacock (Midd), -?-, -?-, Ron Dicks (Midd), Bill Pedley (Northallerton), John Palmer (Northallerton), Val Toase (Easingwold, Northallerton). Front row: Denis Cooper (Northallerton), Brian Clough (Midd) on the grass in front, -?-, -?-, Doug Metcalfe (Northallerton), Derek Stonehouse (Midd), -?-, Bill Hodgson (Northallerton), Nick Merry (Northallerton).

When Yorkshire played Northallerton, who were strengthened by some other local players, in April 1959, they brought their full team – who (with the exception of Fred Trueman) won the County Championship later that year. Fred was resting from cricket after a strenuous tour with England of Australia, but he was in the pavilion at the match recounting stories of the Australian tour so vividly that listeners from both sides were reluctant to go out to bat in case they missed anything! This picture shows Yorkshire CCC. Back row, left to right: Albert Gaskell (Umpire), Jimmy Binks, Ray Illingworth, Don Wilson, Mel Ryan, Brian Stott, Doug Padgett, Ken Palmer (Umpire). Front row: Ron Appleyard, Brian Close, Ron Burnett (Captain), Vic Wilson, Frank Lowson. The team included eight international England players.

The Northallerton XI for the 1959 Yorkshire match is posing in front of the old black tea-hut-cum-bar which saw some convivial social occasions. In 1965 it was replaced by the new pavilion, which was opened with a match against Yorkshire that included Geoff Boycott. Back row, left to right: Albert Gaskell (Umpire), Val Toase (Easingwold), Carlton Forbes (Middlesbro'), Hugh Wrigley, Bill Foord (Scarborough), Brian Bainbridge (Saltburn), Jimmy Cloughton (Scarborough), Mick Riordan, Ken Palmer (Umpire). Front row: John Palmer, John Broadley, Doug Metcalfe (Captain), Ron Diggle, Denis Cooper.

Northallerton Cricket Club Third XI are seen here with the Northallerton and District Evening League Trophy in 1956. They won the trophy several times under the captaincy of Bill Hodgson, combining a blend of youth and experience. Back row, left to right: Chris Merry, Alan Herbert, ? Dunphy, Max Brack, George Gill, David Robinson. Front row: Pat Milner, Harold Bartram, Bill Hodgson (Captain), Denis Beadle, Harry 'Joe' Render. In local sport one generation is often followed by the other in the game and George Gill's son Ian is currently Captain of Northallerton's 1st XI cricket team in the Premier Division of the North Yorkshire South Durham League.

Almost all of Northallerton Cricket Club's playing members assembled in front of the old pagoda pavilion for this photo-call in 1962. Back row, left to right: Ken Palmer (Umpire), Bill Hodgson, Bill Pedley, -?-, Bob Bennison, Doug Burnett, Hugh Wrigley, -?-, Wally Walker, Mike Dillon, Frank Lowther, Roy Peacock, -?-, Alan Pearson, Albert Gaskell (Umpire). Seated: Bob Elgie, Harold Bartram, Les Green, John Broadley, John Palmer, Les Spence, Doug Metcalfe, Harry Burnett. Squatting: -?-, Michael Place, John Raper, John Cooper, Chris Merry, Mike Wake, -?-, -?-.

Northallerton Royal Air Force Association had a strong cricket team in the 1950s and here they are, the winners of the RAFA Durham Region Trophy, the Smales Cup, in 1958. The cup was donated by Mr and Mrs Albert Smales of Northallerton, strong supporters of the RAFA Club there. They were generous sporting philanthropists, supporting many local teams and good causes. Albert was born at the Old Star Inn on the High Street, fought with the Green Howards at the Somme and at Ypres during the First World War, and was the local Northallerton bookmaker. Back row, left to right: Ken Palmer (Umpire), Pete Bateson, George Darwin, Les Green, Denis Beadle, Bill Smith, Roy Peacock, Albert Gaskell (Umpire). Front row: Geoff Milner, Brian Kendrew, Harold Bartram, John Palmer, Tommy Welton.

Another very successful Northallerton-based cricket team was the North Riding NALGO, who won the Yorkshire NALGO Area Trophy – the Shields Memorial Trophy – on several occasions in the 1950s and 1960s. Here is their winning side in 1954. Back row, left to right: Imeson (Umpire), Les Spence, -?-, Brian Husband, Alan Lawson, Frank Lowther, Fred Cowell (Scorer), W. Auton (Umpire). Front row: Alan Pearson, Walter Couling, Ronnie Kettlewell, Denis Cooper, Ray Fawcett, Doug Metcalfe.

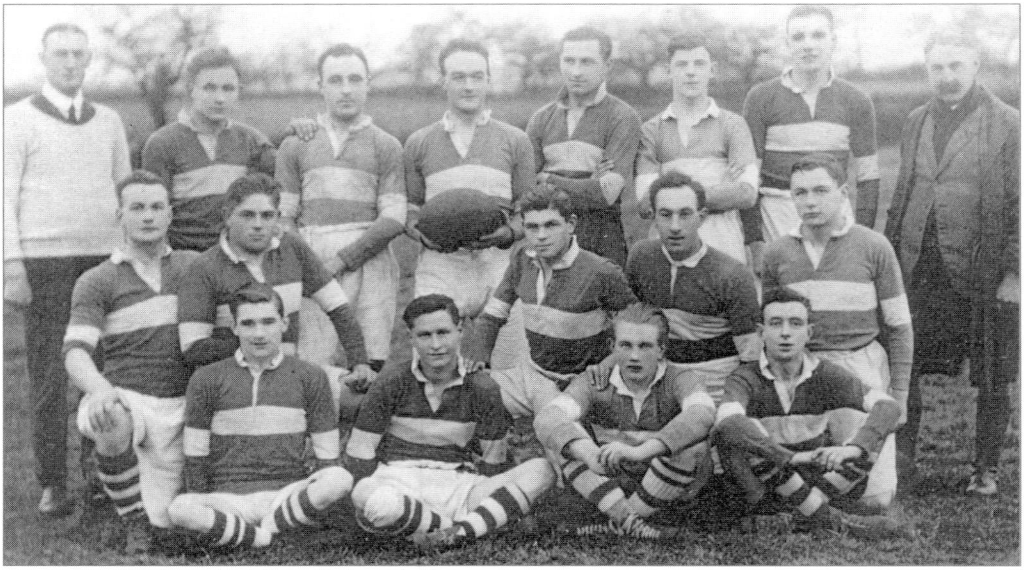

Northallerton Rugby Club, captained by Granville Place, 1927. Granville was the President fifty years later in 1977 when the club won the coveted Yorkshire Silver Trophy. The club was formed in the 1880s and played up Boroughbridge Road when this photograph was taken, Granville's mother Mrs H. Place organised and ran the club. Back row, left to right: A.F. Wagstaff, Richie Pick, J. Hird, L. Atkinson, W.G. Smith, K.C. Calvert, R.V. Metcalfe, R. Booth (Chairman). Middle row: A.W. Watts, H.N. Place, T.W.G. Place, J.L. Swain, W.V. Wrigley. Front row: E.J. Ward, J.B. Place, J. Taylor, J.J. Briggs. Jack Swain and Richie Pick later became chairmen of Northallerton UDC.

Castle Hills FC played between world wars in the Allertonshire League on a field at Harry Carter's Castle Hills Farm, where they changed in a disused cow byre. They are photographed in the 1930/1 season surrounded by their supporters after they had won the Milbank Cup. Some of the team members, identifiable by their football strip, were, back, left to right, H. Greathead, -?-, Alf Glover, -?-, Mike Hogg (bending forward), -?-. Front row: Wilf Norman, Jim Aconley, -?-, Tom Carter, Harry Wilbor.

Northallerton Alliance Juniors were the Milbank Junior Cup Winners in 1949 with this team. Back row, left to right: George Pollard, Pete Derbyshire, Brian Sedgwick, Ian Wallace, Pete Bateson, Brian Colley, John Wilbor. Front row: Keith Wilbor, Derek Smales, Norman Middleton, Derek Fawcett, Alec Greenwood.

Northallerton Alliance Juniors won the Milbank Junior Cup for a third successive year in 1951. Back row, left to right: Don Johnson, Brian Glasper, Brian Sedgwick, Mike Metcalfe, Walter Raine, Mick Riordan. Front row: Peter Dodsworth, Ron Holden, Keith Wilbor, John DiPalma, Dave Pearson.

Northallerton Spartans were formed in 1954 and won their first trophy in 1955, the Thirsk Six-a-Side Cup. This was presented by Sam Bartram, the legendary Charlton Athletic goalkeeper, to Brian Glasper, the Spartans' Captain. Back row, left to right: Maurice Macintosh, Derek Smales, Brian Sedgwick, Brian Glasper, Don Johnson, Ron Holden. Front row: David Simpson, Cec Kyle, Peter Sawdon, Peter Dodsworth.

Northallerton Spartans had their headquarters in the motor bar of the Harewood Arms (now the Tickle Toby) where they repaired every Saturday night in the season. Here the team and some supporters are celebrating on a typical social Saturday evening in 1955: Back row, left to right: Don Cranston, John Palmer, Pete Ingham, Dick Harris, Richard Peacock, John DiPalma, Brian Glasper, Brian Sedgwick, Don Johnson, David Lindop. Front row: Brian Kendrew, Mick Riordan, Doug Lamplough, John Severs, Doug Metcalfe, 'Mazzi' DiPalma.

Northallerton Town had a most successful season in 1956/7, winning three trophies. At that time they also bought the Bluestone Ground, Broomfield, for £1,000, but played at the DMP Ground until Bluestone was properly seeded. The team and officials are shown here. Back row, left to right: Michael Naylor, A. Jack, Reg Mayes, Harry Naylor, Peter Ward, Pete Pearson, Mr Eden. Middle row: Pete Derbyshire, Ron Holden, George Lee, Bernard Bradley, Alan Middlemiss, Brian Ward, Pete Dodsworth, Tom Ward. Front row: Rex Humphries, Dave Robinson, Peter Wilbor, John Ferguson, Ralph Alderson, Stan Durrant, Peter Coulson, Sid Hepplestone.

Northallerton Spartans are seen here before playing Guisborough FC in the North Riding Cup at Stone Cross, on the Allertonshire School east pitch, 1965. Back row, left to right: Cec Kyle, Ernold Cuthbert, John Palmer, Doug Burnett, Brian Kilding. Front row: Colin Hancock, Morgan Atkinson, Pete Sawdon, John Cooper, Alan Gray, Martin Lightfoot.

In 1964 David and William Barker of Northallerton represented Great Britain in the Tokyo Olympic Games in Equestrian Show Jumping Event, with the team narrowly missing out on the medals. They are the only British Olyn representatives so far to have been born in Northallerton (at South Holme, Thirsk Road) and also the first native Northallerton to represent England at international level in sport. They were two of the four children of Northaller born Leslie and Dorothy Barker (née Boston); the others, Anne and Charles, also achieved international show jum status. There are early signs here of parental encouragement, and the attendant jodhpurs and riding hat suggest fut triumphs as the Barker children are captured on the garden steps of their parents' home at Pasture House, Thirsk Rc Northallerton, in 1952. Left to right: David (aged nine), Anne (twelve), Charles (one) and William (six).

This arresting action shot sees the three related Barker Olympic and Great Britain riders airborne and jumping for fun in 1963 down on the farm at Pasture House, Northallerton. In the middle is David Barker of Bilbrough near Leeds who represented Great Britain in the 1960 Rome Olympics Show Jumping. He is the half-cousin of brothers (left) William and (right) David Barker of Pasture House who rode in the 1964 Tokyo Olympics. The latter rode under the name Boston Barker (his full name) to distinguish himself from his older and identically named cousin. In Tokyo in 1964 David rode 'North Riding' and his brother William 'North Flight', both appropriately named in view of their Northallerton connections.

Anne Barker, the eldest child, began the Barker family's show-jumping era by competing in events from an early age. She is here seen winning on 'Lucky Sam' at Southport Show in 1957 when aged eighteen.

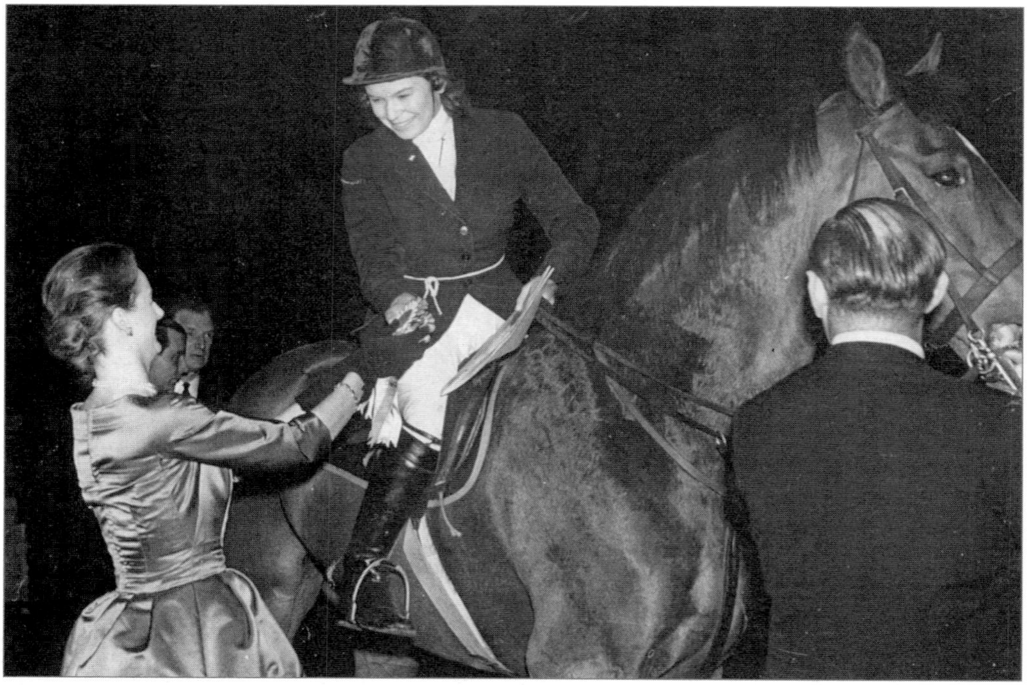

When Anne Barker won the Foxhunter Championship on 7 October 1957 on Lucky Sam at the Horse of the Year Show at Harringay, London, she started the Barkers' international show-jumping success sequence. She is seen here on 'Lucky Sam' at the presentation, receiving the winner's rosette from Mrs Max Aitken, the wife of the editor of the *Daily Express*, the sponsors. Anne was then seventeen, and the event attracted much attention because it was televised in the early days of national television.

David Barker also blossomed early as a show jumper and in 1960, aged seventeen, won two international events in the Horse of the Year Show at Wembley, the Overture Stakes on 'Lucky Joss' and the Dick Turpin Stakes on 'Lucky Sam'. He was Joint Show Jumper of the Year at Wembley with Carole Beard and first represented Great Britain at the Dublin Horse Show in 1962. He continued to represent Great Britain for many years, winning numerous international events. David's sons Ian and Paul carried on the Barker show-jumping tradition and both have represented Great Britain.

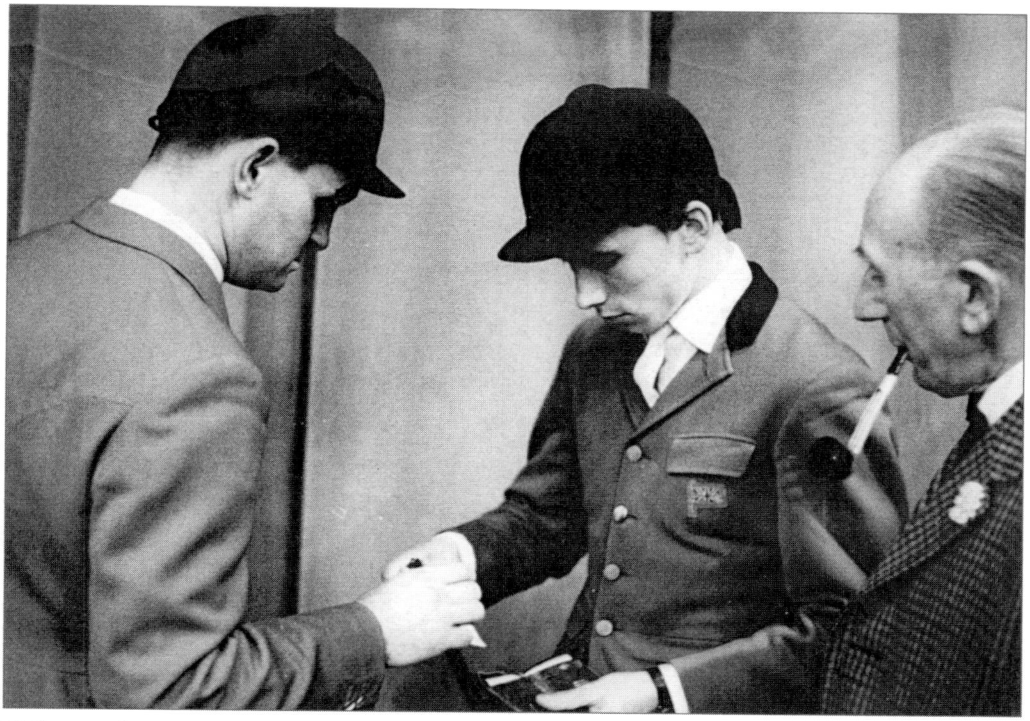

William Barker was just eighteen when he rode in the Tokyo Olympics, having won the Young Riders' Championship of Great Britain at Hickstead in 1963. He then enjoyed a star-studded show jumping career, representing Great Britain often and winning international events at home and in Europe. He was still at the top in 1977 when he was Joint Leading Show Jumper of the Year. This photograph shows William with Harvey Smith and his father Leslie admiring the medal he has just won in Geneva in 1965.

Charles, the youngest of the Barker children, did not stay in show jumping for long but in the short time he did compete he was very skilled and successful. At sixteen he was Young Rider of the Year in 1967 at Wembley and is seen here being presented with the Pontins Trophy for this by Fred Pontin, the sponsor of the competition. Charles went on to win international events such as at the 1970 Horse of the Year Show on 'Vodka' but he soon opted to go into the family business, Barkers of Northallerton, into which he has channelled his entrepreneurial skills as managing director.

A variety of sports clubs and interests have abounded at Northallerton. One of the oldest is the Northallerton Tennis Club which has always been associated with the Northallerton Cricket Club. In 1934 the latter was adjacent to the County Hall on Racecourse Lane where this photograph of Northallerton Tennis Club was taken. It was flourishing and cheerful as this study indicates. Back row, left to right: Teddy Michel, ? Barker, Cyril Ward, Frank Coverdale, Doris Robinson, Harry Wright, Cliff Pearson, Tom Gains. Second row: Delia Lord, Mary Flynn, Joan Shaw, Linda Manging, Freda Woodhead, Gladys Myers. Front row: Dorothy White, Annie Suttill, Mabel Robinson, Olive Challans, Josette ?, Dorothy Woodhead.

Northallerton has had a successful and thriving ladies' hockey team since before the Second World War. This is the 1951 squad photographed at the Knavesmire at York's hockey rally. Back row, left to right: Rhoda Chapman, Mr Barker (Umpire), Essie Meynell, Margaret Blair, Kathleen ?, Christine Waller, Beryl Todd, Dorothy Holmes, Joan Addison, Elsie Hogg. Front row: Margaret Strickland, Sheila Allen, Phyllis Elliot, Brenda Ward, Doreen Mathison, Gladys Plows, Pam Wright.

Badminton was played at various venues in the town and the Zion Badminton Club was very popular. This is the 1952/3 season Junior Club. Back row, left to right: John Coussons, Robert McKenzie, David Severs, Keith Severs, Robert Hardy-King. Front row: Isobel Sherwood, Stewart Walker, J.G. Wilson (Leader), Judith Swan, Barbara Wilson.

Darts has always been one of the most popular pastimes in the area and every Northallerton pub had its own team in the 1950s. One of the most popular sportsmen's pubs was the Harewood Arms with its Newcastle beer and bonhomie. As befitting its sporting image it had a very good darts team, which won the Northallerton Darts League in 1952/3. The winning team is pictured here. Back row, left to right: Jimmy Thompson, Alan Pearson, Harold Bartram, Jimmy Dorling, Wilf Terry, Frank Bartram, Tommy Wilbor. Front row: Les Green, Stan Grainger, Stan Pearson, Arthur Wilson, Doug Fenn, Ernie Nicholson.

There was no athletic club in Northallerton but there was keen interest in athletics in the Grammar and Allertonshire schools; this is the finish of the Northallerton Grammar School senior boys' 100 yards hurdles in 1952 with Brian Glasper (right) going on to win the event and Donald Richardson (left) runner up. Both athletes were also successful at county level. The running track has now been built on, with grammar school/college extensions adjacent to Mill Hill School which was opened in 1956.

Northallerton Automobile Club had an enthusiastic and dedicated following and here at their Dinner Dance and Presentation at the Scotch Corner Hotel in 1963 are some of the annual award winners. Left to right: Robert Edwards, Mercy Beadle, Denis Beadle, Roger Tomlinson, Les Myers, Charles Ashby, Gordon Blakeway.

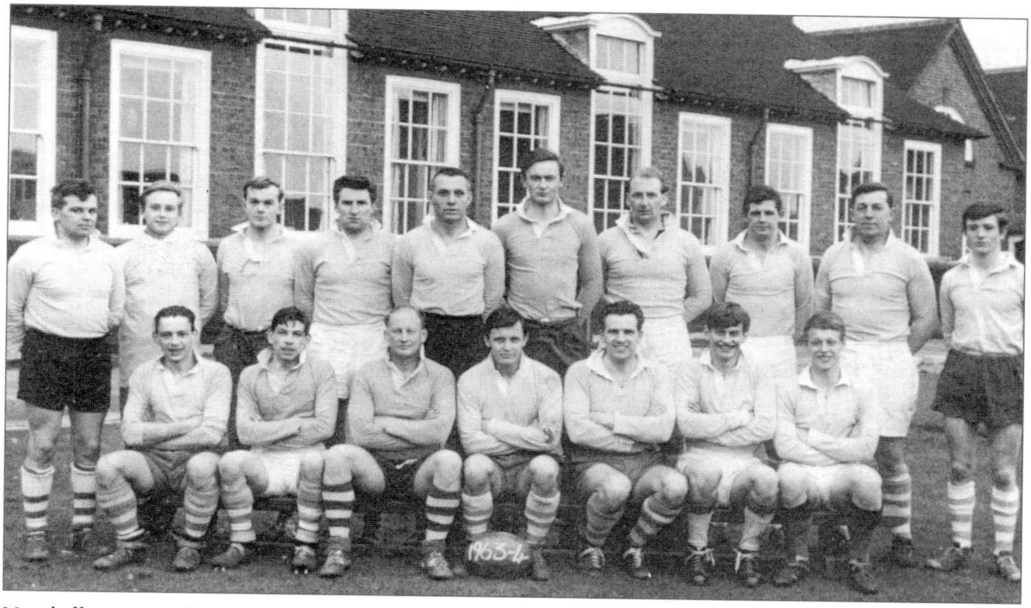

Northallerton Rugby Club was reorganized and reformed after the Second World War and when this photograph was taken at Northallerton Grammar School in 1963 the team was playing at Yafforth Road. Back row, left to right: Jack Whittaker, -?- (an RAF casual), Jeff French, Bill Glover, Bert Pointing, Mike Payton, Jim Bunn, Max Willoughby, Duncan Metcalfe, Ian Porritt. Front row: Keith Place, Clive Place, Dick Lovelace, Peter Jennings, D.M.W. Thomas, Rodney Place, John Murdoch.

Through great endeavours Northallerton Rugby Club moved to its own ground between Stone Cross and Brompton in 1971, but they changed at the West Block in Allertonshire School where this photograph was taken in 1972. In 1974 a new well-appointed club-house was opened at the club's ground, the first function being the post-wedding celebration of Peter Blythe's marriage to Pam Jefferson on 6 July 1974. The club has gone from strength to strength and now boasts four senior teams, a colts fifteen and a thriving junior section. This is the 1972 team. Back row, left to right: -?-, Malcolm Pearson, Bert Langthorne, Dave Robinson, Phil Thompson, John Turner, Stewart Trueman, Rodney Place, Max Willoughby. Front row: John Norwood, Mick Matthews, -?-, Barry Kempen, Mick Castle, Pete Blythe, Dave Bowes.

Ladies' cricket became increasingly popular after the Second World War and this led to the formation of the Northallerton Ladies' Cricket League. One of the teams was Hutton Bonville, seen here in the early 1960s. Back row, left to right: Jean Fletcher, Jean Hatfield, Una Bosomworth, Marjorie Neasome, Edna Rigby, ? Farndale, Jean Jameson. Second row: Audrey Wilkinson, Trixie Turnbull, Mary Langthorne, Sheila Phillips. Front row: Margaret Hill, Edgar Smith, Sybil Phillips.

And where would sport be without the supporters? They are the backbone of every sports club in their behind-the-scenes work, encouragement and basic support. So let them have the last word in this Sports Chapter. They are represented here by Northallerton Middlesbrough Football Club supporters – a loyal, long-suffering and philosophic breed. They are seen in Trafalgar Square before a 'Boro match in London in 1948. Older fans will note the football rattle being waved by Charlie Turner. They are 'Up For 't Cup!' Left to right: Charlie Turner, Allan Rider, Jack Cowell, -?-, Ernest Phillips, Mr Farndale, Fred Rider.

CHAPTER TWELVE

AROUND NORTHALLERTON

Northallerton and the surrounding villages have been interdependent throughout the ages. And in the case of Romanby and Northallerton the two have become literally indivisible. When this exquisite scene at the top of Romanby Green was captured in 1913, with horses predominant and not a car in sight, the village's population was around five hundred and it was still relatively separate from Northallerton. But how times have changed: Romanby's population was 5,333 in 1991 and it is inextricably woven into Northallerton – indeed Northallerton railway station, cricket club and football club, as well as the county hall, are all in Romanby.

Romanby Primary School was opened on its present site in 1953. This is a class of 1959 outside the new school. Back row, left to right: John Edmundson, Paul Rutter, Paul Clarke, Robert Proudlock, John Hogg, Nigel Blagdon, John Jamieson, Robert Pratt. Third row: Glenis Harland, Jean Archer, Lynn MacIntosh, Sandra Vasey, Audrey Foster, Ruth Pinder, -?-, Pamela Nelson, Diana Waddington, Sandra Cardie, Sandra Durham, Kathleen Stubbs. Second row: Rita Brown, Catherine Knowles, Barbara Walters, Elaine Atkinson, Yvonne Lloyd, Karen Dawson, Alexandra Lightfoot, Caroline Steele, Christine Gavin. Front row: Gerald Rennison, Malcolm Robinson, Julien Hird, Barry Nicholl.

The Non Plus at Morton-on-Swale, *c*. 1903. The landlord, G. Atkinson, is just to the left of the door at the back with his wife to his immediate left. Flat caps are definitely in fashion. Several of these gentlemen are anglers as the pub had always been popular with fishermen because of the proximity of the River Swale. The pub has been renamed the Swaledale Arms. The licensed trade evidently runs in the family because Richard Shuttleworth, the Atkinsons' grandson, is mine host at the Odd Fellows Arms, Northallerton.

Dramatic productions often took place in the villages and this is the cast of *Princess Ju Ju*, an operetta performed at Brompton School by a mixed church group from Brompton parish church and the Bethel and Wesley chapels in March 1924. The soloists were Mary Kitching, Alice Burn, Annie Stainthorpe, Herbert Neesam, and Ernest Stainthorpe.

Brompton Whit Sports always brings out the fun and humour of the village. This Fancy Dress line-up in 1960 is a good example. Left to right: Billy Marchant, Vera Robinson, Mary Langthorne, Willie Robinson, Ray Johnson.

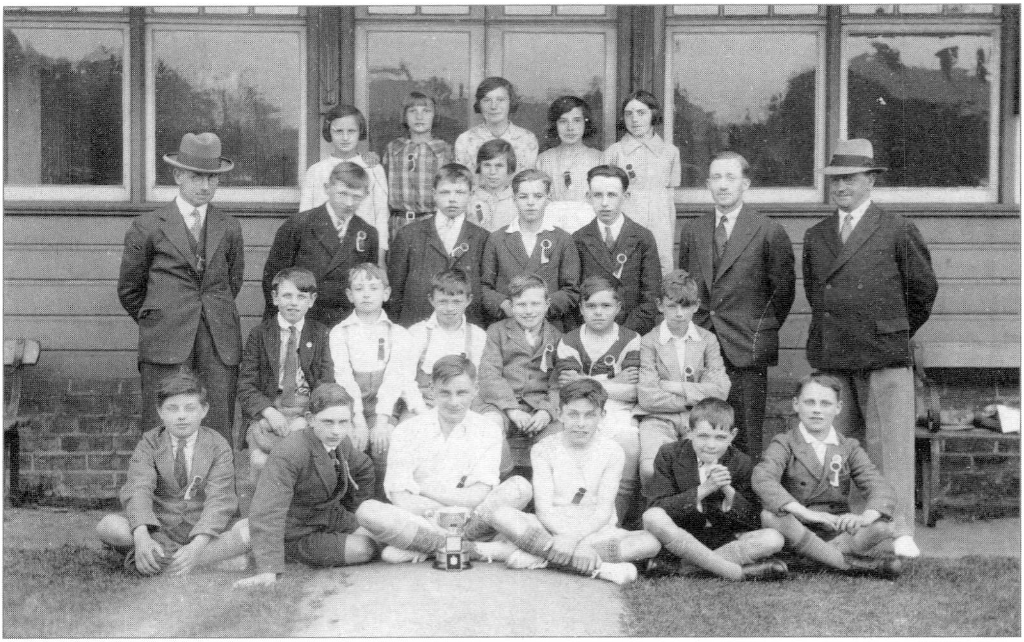

The older pupils of Brompton School pose with some of their elders outside Brompton Cricket Club pavilion in 1927. Back row, left to right: Nancy Walker, Loretta Hoare, Mona Culley, Ivy Gregg, Margaret Goldsborough. Third row: Mr Verrill (schoolmaster), Henry Bowes, John Barker, Tommy Rudd, Ernest Hope, Mr J. Liverseed, Mr Tom Prince (North Riding Physical Education Organizer). Second row: Twaller Bell, Clifford Smith, William Husthwaite, Kenneth Jobling, George Neesom, ? Hill. Front row: Teddy Barker, Fred Alderson, Robert Tutin, Desmond Hoare, Jack Coverdale, Stanley Forth.

This is Brompton Badminton Social Club Dance in the village hall, 22 March 1951. The ladies are having a welcome rest during 'musical chairs.' Left to right: Dolly Winn, Eric Husthwaite, Doug Norman, Norman Burn, Elsie Parrish, Fred Robson, Lucy Smith, Freda Burn, Cec Marchant, Doreen Newcombe (née Forth), Tony Marchant, Margaret Blair, Audrey Oulston, -?-, Keith Wilkinson.

Sport is synonymous with Brompton, and the village cricket team was highly successful in the 1950s. This is the Brompton Cricket XI which played in the Granindon Cup at Northallerton in 1955. Back row, left to right: Dave Kendrew, Frank Robinson, Chris Place, Bert Langthorne, Wilf Terry, John Brown, Trevor Johnson. Front row: Alan Kirby, Danny Kay, Clifford Smith, Les Wetherill.

Country buses were part of rural life and Winn's buses have offered a public service for several decades. Here John Winn the proprietor is photographed with a coach in 1954. Winn Bros is still flourishing.

Thimbleby Cricket Club fielded a formidable village team in the 1950s. They played in the Langbaurgh League. This was the team in the late 1950s, photographed at the Northallerton Cricket Club ground during a Granindon Cup match. Back row, left to right: R. Alderson, B. Ripley, M. Christon, K. Christon, G. Pearson, E. Kendrew. Front row: W. Potter, T. Potter, R. Potter, C. Tate, L. Christon, D. Pollitt (Umpire).

This is an attractive, typically North Yorkshire village scene with Sunday strollers wending through serene Thimbleby, tucked under the Cleveland hills.

Thornton-le-Beans village school was a compact, small but happy place which, like many other village schools, was phased out after 1950 with the North Riding school modernization plan. This delightful photograph of 1929, with the two dogs at the front with the children, gives a nostalgic breath of the closeness and the friendly, secure ambience of this school, set in the peaceful Yorkshire countryside. Back row, left to right: J. Hamilton, -?-, -?-, G. Sanderson, S. Parrott, Robbie Coates, F. Garnin, Tot Coates. Second row: -?-, -?-, -?-, E. Hulley, D. Tennant, V. Parrott, N. Sanderson. Front row: A. Scanlon, M. Scanlon, L. Pearson, K. Scanlon, O. Sanderson, -?-.

Before the introduction of motor transport how did children get to school in Northallerton from the surrounding farms and villages? Well, they either walked or, like Thomas Harker from Pasture House Farm, Kirby Sigston, pictured here in 1893 aged twelve, they went on horseback. Thomas attended Samuel Jackson's West House School at the south end of the Applegarth, Northallerton, and his white pony was stabled nearby during the day – a practice common at Northallerton Grammar School, then adjacent to the parish church.

The 40 mile Lyke Wake Walk across the moors from Ingleby Cross to Ravenscar has been a challenge accepted by numerous people including this group from Northallerton Youth Club in 1956, seen setting off for the overnight hike. Left to right: David Brown, Bob Bennison, Nita Kitching, Daphne Beames, Brian Cotton, Brenda Piggins, Ken Richardson. The four young men were among the first six finishers out of a total of thirty-four starters, and they covered the distance in 16 hours and 20 minutes.

Osmotherley is inextricably linked with the Lyke Wake Walk and over the decades it has become a centre for walkers and support groups. Set at the foot of the Hambleton hills this village of Saxon origin is so idyllic that it is a constant attraction both to tourists and to those nearer at hand in North Yorkshire and Teesside. John Wesley was so captivated by Osmotherley that he stayed there on over a dozen occasions from the 1750s onwards. The scene has changed little since this photograph was taken in about 1900, with the solid cross a reminder of pleasant days to many thousands.

Scruton Cricket Club was so successful in the 1950s that it won the Northallerton Evening League every year from 1955 to 1958 playing in the attractive setting of Scruton Hall grounds. The team is pictured here with the trophy on one of those celebratory occasions. Back row, left to right: Charlie Hoare, Jack Bell, Ernie Smith, Eric Woodburn, Harold Robinson, Pete Bateson, Les Green, Noel Green, James French. Front row: Tony Plews, Bill Harrison, Albert Dale, Jack Watson, Les Bell.

Ainderby village school has always had an excellent reputation, as it did when this photograph was taken in 1939 at the old school in the girls yard. Charles Bateson, who won the Military Medal with the Black Watch at the Somme in 1916, was the long-serving headmaster. There are two classes here of eight to ten year olds, and they include many well known personalities. Back row, left to right: Sheila Carter, Ken Horn, Les Harland, Bernard Peacock, Dawn Bailey. Third row: Pete Bateson, Alan Lowes, Esme Atkinson, Greta Herring, Rita Rowntree, Rachel Robinson, June Winspeare, ? Parker, Sheila Pearson, -?-, Janet Simpson, Zena Hall. Second row: Jean Rowntree, Jean Harland, Nita Webster, Margaret Webster, Gwen Watson, Judy Bailey. Front row: Eric Harland, Morris Pearson, Harry Atkinson, Robert Phillips, Malcolm Dillon, Ted Edwards, Geoff Hall, Godfrey Knapton, -?-, Maureen Simpson.

For many years village women's institutes have been a byword for local enterprise, social organization, village presentation and promotion, and supporters of charities and good works. Representing all of these in the Northallerton area are Danby Wiske WI in the early 1950s, pictured in the village hall which was a Nissen hut. Standing, include: Mrs Severs, Mrs Jobling, Mrs Fishburn, Mrs Middlemiss, Mrs Barker, Mrs Stevenson, Mrs Armstrong. Seated, left to right: Mrs Rayfield, Mrs Joan Stevens, Miss Dorrington, Mrs Bellwood, Mrs Husband.

This animated action scene of the end of a wheelbarrow race is typically village sports day or show day vintage when good fun was had by all, with all the village joining in and contributing. This is Danby Wiske sports day in 1946, revived thankfully after the Second World War. The lone car is reminiscent of earlier motoring days.

No description of Northallerton would be complete without a reference to its nearest market town, Bedale, with which it has developed through the ages, enjoying many links – historical, commercial, sporting, family and personal. The ancient church of St Gregory is of Saxon origin and has one of the best examples of a fortified tower in the North of England; it stands stately in the background as a reminder of Bedale's antiquity. In modern times, this is the exact scene shown in the famous film *The Way to the Stars* in 1944 with John Mills and Michael Redgrave.

Edwin Kitching of Thornton-le-Moor epitomizes those country folk of the whole area who have fashioned it, given it its character and created its history – because history is basically about people. Edwin was a man of the soil who lived to over ninety in his beloved North Yorkshire, except for his time spent on the Western Front fighting for his country in the First World War. Sturdy, strong, contented, jocund, hard-working and in love with the very basics of nature, this simple study says things that words cannot about 'the fair North Riding'.

ACKNOWLEDGEMENTS

Dorothy Alderson · Rita Banks · Charles Barker · David Barker · George Barker William Barker · Olga and Harold Bartram · Kay and Ron Bateson · Marjorie and Peter Bateson · Peter Blythe · Mercy and Denis Beadle · Sheila Braithwaite · Colin Burn Barbara and David Carr · Alan Carter · Grace Carter · Joan and Barry Cawthorne Lol Christon · Katherine Cooper · Mrs E. Cornforth · Valerie Corns · Celia Coulthard Dorothy Dewar · Brenda Dodsworth · Nicola Fois · David Gamble · Brian Glasper Mike Green · Brian Hill · Mrs A.C. Horner · Ivan Humphrey · Geoff Husband · Nancy Hutchinson · Doreen Jarvis · Alan Joyce and L. Bell · Audrey and Bill Kitching · Bert and Mary Langthorne · Jean and Tony MacLean · Linda McMaster · Doug Metcalfe · Pat Mitchell · Doreen Newcombe · Marion Norwood · John Palmer · Arnold Pearson Walter Raine · Joyce Render · Keith Richardson · Greta Rider · Jean Robinson Mrs R. Robinson · Elaine Sayer · Jim Sedgwick · Richard Shuttleworth · Anne Smirthwaite · B. Spence · Brian Stockdale · Brian Taylor · Dorothy Thompson · Harry Thompson · Mrs F. Tyreman · Phil Wayman · John Wilbor · John Willis · Olga Wilson Pat Woodall.

For the courtesy afforded and provision of reference facilities:

North Yorkshire Reference Library, Northallerton · North Yorkshire County Record Office, Northallerton · Darlington Local History Library · British Library, London · Christ Church College, Oxford · The Public Record Office, Kew.
Anne Smirthwaite for invaluable administrative assistance and computer transcription.